Greenhouse gardening

Lovell Benjamin

Edited for U.S. Greenhouse Owners
By Marjorie Dietz

Floraprint

Published 1977 by Floraprint Limited,
Park Road, Calverton, Nottingham.
Designed and produced for Floraprint by
Intercontinental Book Productions
Copyright © 1977 Intercontinental Book Productions
and Floraprint Limited. North American edition
Copyright © 1981 Intercontinental Book Productions and
Floraprint U.S.A.

ISBN 0-938804-08-1

Design by Design Practitioners Limited

Photographs supplied by Floraprint Limited (copyright
I.G.A.), Humex, Halls Homes and Gardens, Harry Hebditch,
Baco Leisure Products, Harry Smith, N.H.P.A., Spectrum
Colour Library, Bernard Alfieri

Printed in U.S.A.

Contents

1 Why grow plants under glass?   4

2 Types of greenhouse   5

3 Choosing a greenhouse   9

4 Installing a greenhouse   10

5 Running a greenhouse   12

6 Greenhouse equipment   17

7 Greenhouse culture   22

8 Growing vegetables under glass   26

9 Growing fruit under glass   30

10 Growing plants under glass   34

11 Frames and other plant protectors   56

12 Common greenhouse pests and diseases   61

Index   64

1 Why grow plants under glass?

Nowadays a greenhouse is essential for the complete gardener. One of its most important assets is that it makes possible substantial economies in household budgets: ordinary fruits and vegetables can be grown both in and out of season, and more exotic items – usually expensive in the shops – can also be produced at low cost. Seedlings and cuttings can be raised by the gardener himself, reducing annual expenditure on garden plants, and giving him the satisfaction of creating something more or less from nothing. What is more, the protection given by greenhouses against outdoor weather conditions allows many tender decorative plants to be grown, which will give enthusiasts increased pleasure.

Right: Greenhouse gardening provides an opportunity to grow a wide variety of colorful plants, such as the orange-flowered *Streptosolen jamesonii* shown here.

Below: The pendulous flowers of fuchsias provide beautiful summer flower displays in greenhouses.

2 Types of greenhouse

Before buying a greenhouse, look at several types and decide what sort suits your purposes best. They are usually classified according to use – and by size, shape or construction materials. The temperature and degree of humidity at which the greenhouse is to be maintained determine the type of plants that can be grown in it and also, in a general sense, the purpose for which the greenhouse will be used. Experts usually refer to greenhouses in the following ways.

Cold greenhouse This type depends entirely on the heat of the sun for warmth, and it is therefore most valuable in the spring, summer and autumn. The great disadvantage of the cold greenhouse is that it affords little protection against severe frost and is therefore not able to protect tender plants in winter unless the season is exceptionally mild.

Cool greenhouse In many ways a cool greenhouse is the most useful type for most gardeners. During the summer, when unheated, it fulfills the function of a cold greenhouse. During the spring, autumn and winter it is heated enough to maintain a night temperature of 45°F (7°C). This is sufficient to keep out the frost and so allows many tender plants to be overwintered, together with, for example, dahlias and begonia tubers. A cool greenhouse can also be used for raising many kinds of plants from seed.

Intermediate or warm greenhouse This is the type that true gardening enthusiasts, eager to extend the interest and scope of their hobby, will wish to acquire. With all the many very valuable practical aspects listed above, the warm greenhouse combines the advantage of enabling such commodities as tomatoes and cucumbers to be grown together with some of the more exotic fruits and vegetables – such as eggplants, figs, avocados, peaches and nectarines. Warm greenhouses are heated to a minimum night temperature of 55°F (13°C) which makes it possible to grow decorative house plants and to carry out propagation.

Tropical or hot house This type, perhaps more for the connoisseur than the ordinary gardener, used to be called a stove house and the plants grown in it, stove plants. Heated to a night temperature of about 65°F (18°C) and kept very humid, it can be used for growing certain kinds of orchids, maidenhair ferns, fittonias, caladiums, and many gesneriads. Many tropical plants, however, adapt readily to the warm greenhouse. Like the warm house, the hot house is useful for propagation, especially when a high temperature is essential.

Dieffenbachia needs a warm, humid atmosphere and so is best grown in a tropical or hot house.

Greenhouse shapes

Physically, greenhouses are classified by their shape, which to some extent determines their function. The common ones are listed below.

Span or ridge This is the most popular type. It has a roof in the form of an inverted shallow V and the more conventional type has vertical glass sides, although there is now a tendency to produce this type with glass panels set at an angle of about 10° to the vertical. It is claimed that this provides greater resistance to crosswinds and a greater stability; greenhouses built in this way require less bracing, and there is better light transmission.

If mainly ground crops (such as lettuce, chrysanthemums and tomatoes) are to be grown, span greenhouses, in common with some other types, are glazed to the ground. If pot plants are to be the specialty, the glazing is usually supported on a bench-high wall of brick, concrete, wood or metal.

Three-quarter span This type of greenhouse is built against a wall. It has an inverted V-shape roof, but the span on the wall side is shorter than the other, which is of normal length. This type has an advantage over a standard lean-to (see below) in that it gives more light and headroom, but it is more costly. One of the best uses of this greenhouse is to grow fruit on the wall side and display plants on the opposite side.

Lean-to The lean-to has a single sloping roof and is built against a wall. It is the least expensive to buy and heat, and indeed, can often be heated from the house system. Its disadvantage is that plants grown in it tend to bend towards the light.

Circular This is among the latest ideas in greenhouses, and includes geodesic dome models. It is excellent for pot plants and cultivation. However, extractor fans usually need to be installed to prevent overheating in hot weather.

Above: A three-quarter span greenhouse has the virtues of the lean-to type but has the advantage of giving more light and height.

Left: This span, or ridge, greenhouse is glazed to the base, making it valuable for growing ground crops such as chrysanthemums, lettuce and tomatoes.

Right: A lean-to greenhouse can be very useful, especially where space is restricted. As it is built against a wall, it is suitable for fruit.

Mini For gardeners with only a very small space to spare, a miniature greenhouse could be the answer. Some are free-standing, while others 'lean-to' against a wall or extend from a window. This type of greenhouse, though small, can fulfill many of the functions of a full-size greenhouse.

Conservatory This is essentially a greenhouse that is accessible from a living room, to which it can be a pleasing adjunct. Filled with exotic plants, it makes a restful extra room in both summer and winter, combining the atmosphere of the garden with the comfort of light and heat from the house supply.

Above: Both the ridge and lean-to types of miniature greenhouse are invaluable to those with little space.

Below: The attractive design of this circular greenhouse allows it to be positioned anywhere.

Above: A conservatory makes an excellent and very useful extension to a living room.

Construction materials

The relative merits of the various materials used in constructing greenhouses are listed below.

Wood This is warm and relatively easy to work. The strongest is teak, and redwood is very popular. Both need oiling, and the latter is more easily worked. Other woods used include cypress and pine that has been salted. The cheaper woods must be painted regularly.

Metal (steel and aluminum) Steel needs painting, but aluminum does not. Aluminum alloys are strong, and although light they stand firm provided the greenhouse itself is firmly sited. The metal frame must be rigid and include provision for expansion and contraction to avoid glass breakage and air leakage.

Concrete Reinforced concrete is usually used for greenhouses, and although not as attractive as some other materials, concrete does provide a very durable structure.

A greenhouse constructed of red cedar requires treatment with linseed oil annually.

Glazing: glass v. plastic Glass has long been a very satisfactory glazing material, but plastic-glazed greenhouses have recently become very popular. There is a fairly wide selection from which to choose among the plastics.

The cheapest is polyethylene, which is very easy to install. Its main disadvantages are: it is weathered by sun (this is slowed down by specifying ultraviolet resistant) and torn by wind, reducing its life span to about two years; it can become dirty and cannot be cleaned the way glass can; and also condensation is greater, although powered fans can be installed to reduce this problem.

More expensive and much longer-lived are the rigid fiberglass panels, which retain heat better than polyethylene. Also coming into use is acrylic, but it is usually more expensive than glass. It scratches, but it is clear and can be molded into curves. None of the plastics shatters like glass.

3 Choosing a greenhouse

Buying a greenhouse is an investment, so before you purchase one decide on the way you intend to use it. This, of course, depends entirely on the type of crops that are to be grown. For ground crops, such as chrysanthemums and lettuce, the greenhouse will need glazing right down to the base. Flowering pot plants and propagation call for benches, in which case the glazing can be fixed to basal walls 2–3 ft (60–100 cm) high, and heat loss will be reduced. If both types are to be cultivated, a greenhouse glazed to the ground on one side, with a bench and wall on the other, will fit the bill. With restricted space, or if wall-fruits are to be grown, a lean-to is the best proposition.

If it is the gardener's intention to cultivate plants that need heat, the most economic construction in this respect should be chosen. It is also as well to visualize the possibility of any future expansion that may be required.

Size

Although the choice of greenhouse will depend upon the gardener's pocket, it is a great mistake to buy one that is too small.

Above: This greenhouse is only 8 ft (2·5 m) by 6 ft (2 m) yet has ample headroom and good space for staging.

Left: A greenhouse must have a door wide enough to take a wheelbarrow comfortably.

In any case, a small greenhouse is difficult to manage – it warms up too quickly in summer and cools too fast in winter. A greenhouse must have adequate headroom and, ideally, be wide enough to allow for a wheelbarrow to pass through the door. (It is important to ensure that the door opens inwards, or slides easily backwards and forwards.) Another inconvenience of too narrow a house is that it will not allow for a wide enough path, or adequate width to the benches. A good minimum size is about 8 ft (2·5 m) wide by 6 ft (2m) long.

4 Installing a greenhouse

Siting

Careful attention should be paid to choice of location. The site should be level, if it is not, it should be leveled. It should be well-drained, sheltered from strong and cold winds and should receive plenty of sunshine. The position chosen will of course be influenced, particularly in a small garden, by miscellaneous factors such as existing paths, boundary fences, the situation of the house, etc., but the above criteria are ideal, and will also determine the direction in which the greenhouse should run. The best position is running north and south, to afford the maximum amount of light throughout the year. However, if the greenhouse is to be used largely for raising seedlings and propagating plants in winter, an east-to-west direction will give maximum light at that time of year. A lean-to should preferably be erected facing south. A conservatory is best positioned so that it forms an extension to the living room and has direct access from it.

It is also important to position the greenhouse where water, gas and electricity supplies are available, or where they can easily be made so.

Note Greenhouses above a certain size, stipulated by the zoning laws in each area, may require planning permission. Before committing yourself to buying and erecting a greenhouse, it is as well to check this point, and also to consult with neighbors regarding the proposed position of the greenhouse.

Laying foundations and paths

A path of concrete slabs or coal ashes or bricks can be laid through the center of the greenhouse. It is also advantageous to lay a path giving access from the house.

Good foundations are essential to eradicate the risk of movement, and consequent glass breakage. Solid foundations also provide good anchorage. Greenhouse makers always provide a foundation plan prior to delivery, and some also sell suitable ready-made foundations.

In aluminum greenhouses the weight to be supported is fairly low, so the foundations need not be as heavily constructed, but must still provide a firm base.

A suitable foundation for a greenhouse glazed to the ground can be provided by digging a trench 10 in (25 cm) deep by 1 ft

Left: A modern conservatory with direct access from a living room is ideal for house plants.

Right: Erecting a greenhouse.
(1) These two drawings show typical foundations, the first for a greenhouse glazed to the ground, the second for one with a bench-high base wall, supporting a glazed superstructure.
(2) Positioning the sides.
(3) Putting on the roof.
(4) When glazing, use putty for wood frames and plastic sealing compound for metal frames.

(30 cm) wide with vertical sides. In this, a brick or concrete footing should be built. If the superstructure is to be supported on brick or concrete block walls, the top of the foundation, which in this case might be a filling of concrete, should be 6 in (15 cm) below ground level. Provide for plumbing and electricity before the concrete is put in.

Erection

Greenhouse manufacturers always supply very complete directions for the erection of their products. The work usually consists of bolting prefabricated parts together, and calls for few tools other than wrenches, screwdrivers, and perhaps a masonry drill. For glazing, use putty in a wooden greenhouse, elastic sealing compound in a metal one. Manufacturers will also erect greenhouses themselves.

Maintenance

The most important tasks are as follows:
(1) Occasionally treat wood by wiping it with a rag dipped in linseed oil.
(2) Unless allowing it to weather, treat red cedar with a cedar preservative.
(3) Regularly paint softwood and steel. (Aluminum needs no painting.)
(4) Wash glass regularly, removing moss, etc., by scraping and hosing down.
(5) Scrub and whitewash walls annually.
(6) Paint heating pipes with aluminum paint. Do not, however, use creosote on the staging, etc., inside the greenhouse, it emits fumes that are toxic to plants.

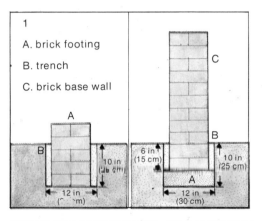

1
A. brick footing
B. trench
C. brick base wall

2

3

4

5 Running a greenhouse

Ventilation

No matter what the type of greenhouse – cold, cool, warm or tropical – ventilation is most important because it controls heat and humidity, and helps avoid such disorders as 'damping off', which can have a disastrous effect. In a well-designed greenhouse there are ventilators, i.e. fanlights that open, on either side of the roof, and one in each side panel. Normally, one set is provided for each 10 ft (3 m) run of length. Some greenhouses are fitted with louver ventilators in the sides. These provide ventilation that can be very finely controlled. Ventilators on the leeward side can be opened when it is windy without causing any cold drafts. In warm weather they may be opened on both sides to reduce the temperature, control humidity and admit fresh air to the plants.

Ventilation in greenhouses demands considerable attention, and for this reason automatic methods of control have been developed. One of them is a simple device that is fitted on to each ventilator to open and shut it automatically. It does this by

virtue of a cylinder filled with a mineral substance that expands or contracts with variations in temperature. The device is very sensitive, easy to fit and comparatively inexpensive.

A second method of automatic ventilation control is to use an electric fan controlled by a thermostat. Fans are normally fitted in the gable end of the greenhouse.

Above: Careful attention must be paid to ventilating a greenhouse. An automatic ventilating fan, which is thermostatically controlled, can be fitted in the gable end of the greenhouse. Sometimes a fan is operated in conjunction with a louver fitted on the outside of the mounting panel.

Left: An alternative method of ventilation is a mechanical system that automatically opens or shuts as necessary.

Shading

Shading is another way of effectively cutting down the heat in a greenhouse, and is used in conjunction with ventilation. It is particularly valuable for certain pot plants, early propagation and tomatoes suffering from verticillium wilt. Shading can be done in the following ways.

(1) The glass on the outside can be painted with well-diluted emulsion paint, a lime and water mixture or a proprietary shading.

Such shading is effective during the summer but should be progressively washed off by winter, when all the available light is needed.

(2) Blinds, either of the venetian or the roller type, can be fitted either inside or outside; the outside type of blind is better because the sun's rays should ideally be checked before they reach the glass. There is one type of blind made from unplasticized vinyl tubes, which, if they are rolled down at nightfall during winter, minimize fuel consumption in a heated greenhouse.

Shading from the hot sun is important for keeping down the temperature in a greenhouse and these external blinds made from unplasticized vinyl tubes can also reduce heat loss in winter.

In some cases roller blinds fitted inside can be automatically controlled by means of a thermostat or photoelectric cell.

(3) Sun vizors, in which the blinds are held rigid at the correct slope for the roof of the greenhouse, can be used. They can be controlled by an electronic eye, and are among the most efficient types of shading.

Vinyl blinds are excellent for shading from the sun.

Heating

Heating a greenhouse is by no means cheap, and in the long run the final decision will depend on which fuel is cheapest and how easily a supply can be provided for the greenhouse. The choice must remain an individual one, but if, for example, the rate for your house gas supply is cheaper than other forms of power, then quite obviously this is the one that should be given the first consideration. The various alternatives are considered below.

Hot-water pipes This is the traditional method of heating a greenhouse, but it necessitates the installation of a boiler and hot-water pipes, which are usually placed under the staging. Formerly, such a boiler was fired with solid fuel, usually coke, but today gas, oil or electricity are more usual. The advantage of these is that any system

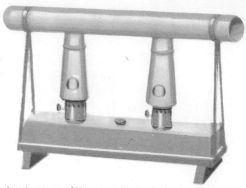

Another type of Kerosene heater is the double-burner heater illustrated above.

using them can be fully automatic. Two advantages of hot-water pipes are that they distribute the heat uniformly and retain their heat for some time.

If the home system has enough spare capacity it may be possible to heat the greenhouse from that.

Electric heaters Although heating by electricity is costly, it has a number of advantages in greenhouses. It is clean and always reliable unless there are power cuts. With thermostats of a correct and trustworthy design, control of the greenhouse temperature can be more precise than with any other form of heating. However, once the power is cut off cooling down will take place, except where night storage heaters are used – but with these there are problems of temperature control, therefore they are not highly recommended. (When buying your greenhouse, discuss with the salesman recommendations for emergency heaters to use when there is a power failure in your region during freezing weather.)

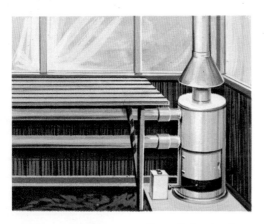

Above: Hot-water pipes are a long-established method of heating greenhouses.

Left: Kerosene heaters, such as the single burner heater illustrated here, are popular on the Continent.

The types of electrical equipment more usually installed for greenhouse heating are fan heaters, and tubular heaters.

Fan heaters are extremely efficient electric heaters for a greenhouse. They are usually light, 4–5 lbs (2–2·5 kg) and are quite portable, so that they can be positioned anywhere – however, they are most usually placed in the center of the floor. Their great asset is that they maintain a gentle movement of air, which is appreciated by plants and encourages growth. Fan heaters work on the principle of sucking in cold air at one end, warming it and blowing it out at the other. This heated air rises naturally by convection, circulates, cools and then falls to the ground again, where it is reheated. Fan heaters are thermostatically controlled, but even when the heating elements are switched off, the fan keeps the air gently circulating.

The great qualities of tubular heaters are their long life, almost negligible maintenance costs, their comparatively low initial cost and their adaptability. They are best fitted singly or in banks against the wall of the greenhouse.

Tubular heaters can, however, get very hot and scorch plants close to them unless they are thermostatically controlled. This also ensures, of course, the current is used only when necessary, and at the same time automatically maintains the required minimum temperature.

For safety reasons, it is a wise precaution to mount tubular heaters on wooden supports when installing in a metal greenhouse.

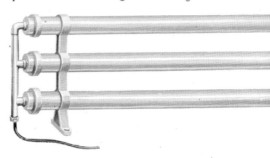

A bank of electric tubular heaters provides a clean, controllable, reliable and flexible form of heating.

Electric fan heaters can be wall-mounted (*top*) or floor-standing (*above*). With or without thermostatic control, they are very convenient.

Gas heaters When burned, gas derived from coal gives off chemicals that are detrimental to plants, but the products of natural-gas combustion are beneficial, especially the carbon dioxide that enters the air. Natural-gas burning apparatus is now available for greenhouse heating. Such apparatus is easily placed below the staging and connected to the gas source by means of a flexible pipe. Burners can have thermostatic control and be fitted with a flame-failure device as a safety precaution.

For the running of a gas burner there must be adequate air to burn the fuel. Usually, this requirement is adequately met by the normal leakage in a greenhouse. If there is any problem, an air brick in the foundation wall above ground level will solve it. Lastly, note that a gas heater may be unsuitable for a plastic greenhouse because of the condensation caused, which is heavier than that brought about by electrical heaters.

Heat conservation

No doubt double glazing would reduce the heat losses in a greenhouse. However, the cost of hermetically sealing together two

A thermostat is invaluable for controlling the temperature in an electrically heated greenhouse.

sheets of glass is high, and it would be prohibitively expensive to double glaze an ordinary home greenhouse.

Heat losses and drafts can, however, be reduced by lining the greenhouse inside with thin polyethylene, leaving the vents, of course, uncovered. Lining will increase the humidity, so careful attention to ventilation will be needed afterwards.

Control Equipment

Through the advent of more efficient heating and ventilation equipment for the amateur greenhouse enthusiast, precision control equipment is now available for all greenhouses. This can be used to open and close ventilators, operate heaters, and activate propagation units.

The ventilator-opening units have proved to be invaluable to the amateur. Ventilators can be made to open and close at exactly the correct time in relation to the temperature of the air within the greenhouse, and not when it suits the owner. These units rely on the expansion of a sub-stance, which, when warmed by the temperature within the greenhouse, expands and forces a piston to open the ventilators.

Greenhouse heaters can be linked to thermostats which switch on the heater. The exact temperature at which the heater operates can be adjusted according to the hardiness of the plants within the greenhouse. However, ensure that an excessive temperature is not given, as this may damage the plants and be very costly. Use this in conjunction with a minimum and maximum temperature thermometer, so that you can check that the heating is operating at the correct temperature and not wasting energy.

Propagation units set in a greenhouse can be effectively heated by electricity at a very reasonable cost. A thermostat operates to prevent the soil temperature rising too high, or becoming cold. Mist propagation units are controlled by moisture-sensing units, as described earlier.

6 Greenhouse equipment

Benches and shelves

Staging is an important and valuable part of greenhouse equipment. Benches are essential when a greenhouse is to be used primarily for growing flowering pot and house plants, especially when they are displayed for their beauty. Benches are also very valuable for raising plants from seeds or rooting cuttings in boxes or pots; ideally, the benches should be slatted, to allow warm air to rise up through them from the heaters below and thus provide bottom heat. The dark place under the benches in a greenhouse with basal walls can be used for storage or for such purposes as blanching endives and forcing rhubarb.

Often made of red cedar or softwood, benches or staging in a greenhouse gives more space.

Benches are usually fitted 30–34 in (75–85 cm) above floor level – a comfortable working height. If possible, they should be 3–3½ ft (90–105 cm) wide. Whether slatted or solid, they should be fitted away from the wall, to allow for air circulation. The materials most commonly used are wood (redwood), particularly when the benches are slatted, Transite (a cement product that won't rot), and hardware cloth (heavy wire with a small mesh).

Shelves are of great value in a greenhouse, and should be of similar construction. They are very useful for keeping plants near the light, especially in winter.

Aluminum shelves, fixed above the staging to the greenhouse structure, are a great asset.

They are particularly valuable for displaying pendulous plants, such as cascade chrysanthemums. If of softwood, benches and shelves must be kept regularly painted.

Watering

Systematic watering is essential to all kinds of plants grown in a greenhouse.

Watering by hand For this task it is important to have a watering-can with a long spout fitted with a fine rose that delivers a gentle stream of water, particularly when seeds, seedlings and small cuttings are being handled. There are several good ones available from nursery supply houses. The best, unfortunately, are expensive, as they are imported.

When watering by hand it is of great value to use a moisture indicator (available from many nursery supply firms), which takes much of the guesswork out of the task.

Automatic watering Watering by hand can be a hard and inconvenient chore, yet to fail to water, even once, might result in disaster. Fortunately, automatic watering systems, not too expensive and quite easy to install, are now available.

A very good type is a capillary system, which allows plants in pots to keep themselves automatically supplied with their requirements of water. The pots, which should not be crocked, are stood on a suitable substance which is usually sand and which is contained in a specially constructed fiberglass tray on the bench, or on a capillary fiber mat laid out on a plastic sheet directly on the staging. In either case, there is a supply trough that overhangs the front edge of the staging and is kept filled with water. The water is absorbed continuously by the sand or base material. In the case of the sand tray, this absorption is achieved by means of a fiberglass wick partially buried in the sand with its ends in the water. The capillary mat, on the other hand, is cut to shape so that a tongue can be inserted in the trough.

With automatic watering equipment, water is transferred from a tank to the sand on which the plants are standing.

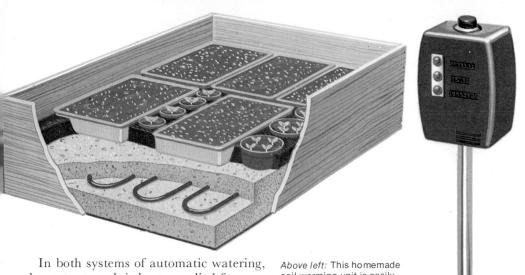

In both systems of automatic watering, the water trough is kept supplied from an overhead tank or an inverted gallon jar (4·5 liters), which can be refilled periodically. If, however, mains water is turned on, the system can be made fully automatic by means of a ball valve and float.

Above left: This homemade soil-warming unit is easily constructed. It is essential for the propagation of certain plants and lowers running costs.

Above right: A moisture indicator minimizes the risk of plant fatalities caused by drying out or overwatering.

Soil warming

Soil warming is a very useful and inexpensive modern greenhouse technique. By warming the soil in the borders or on the benches, it is possible to increase the range of heat-loving plants that can be grown. It is also of the greatest use in seed germination, rooting cuttings and producing out-of-season vegetables and fruits. This can all be done without raising the temperature of the whole greenhouse.

Warming cables can be bought in lengths and watts ranging from 20 ft (6 m), carrying 75 watts, which will heat 10–12 sq ft (0·9–1·1 sq m) to 267 ft (82 m), carrying 1000 watts, suitable for a surface of 133–166 sq ft (12·5–15 sq m). The soil-warming system is quite easy to install. However, if you are inexperienced in such matters, you should seek the help of a qualified electrician for connection of the cables to the mains supply. First, place a sheet of asbestos or roofing felt on the bench and erect 9 in (22·5 cm) wooden walls

around it. In the bottom of this enclosure, put a 2 in (5 cm) layer of coarse washed river sand. The warming cable is laid on this base, running evenly backwards and forwards. It is then covered with a further 2–3 in (5–7·5 cm) of sand. The seed pans or boxes are stood on this sand. To ensure a uniform temperature throughout the bed, pack granulated peat in the spaces between the seed containers. If desired, part or the whole of the sand bed can be covered with a mixture of peat and sand and the cuttings to be rooted can be inserted directly into it.

If it is necessary to warm the air around the plants, a similar warming cable can be run round the walls, and the bed covered with a sheet of glass or plastic.

Generally, if the power is switched on for ten to twelve hours each night, all the heat needed is given. If completely automatic control is desired, a soil-warming thermostat should be fitted. Ready-wired units can be purchased.

Propagation units

Propagation units are useful devices, particularly for rooting cuttings. To succeed in getting roots to grow on a short length of stem it is necessary to keep the stem perfectly healthy and the tissues active; if it flags in any way, rooting is not likely to take place. If, however, the process is allowed to take place in a propagation case, the temperature and humidity will be higher than if it occurs out in the open greenhouse. In consequence, the tissues of the leaves and stems remain moist and the rooting process is accelerated.

Two very simple forms of propagating case are, firstly, a seed box covered with a sheet of glass and, secondly, a plastic bag enveloping a seed pan or a pot. The more highly developed propagation units are based on the elementary principle embodied in these two devices.

A propagating case has numerous uses. In the first place, it allows a cold

greenhouse to be used for raising seeds and rooting cuttings with little extra expenditure on fuel. It also enables an earlier start to be made with raising seeds, which results in earlier crops in the greenhouse – for example, tomatoes. Flowers, normally produced from seeds planted during the summer for the following year, need not be exposed to severe winter weather. They can be sown in January in a propagator to produce better summer results. If a propagation unit is used in a heated greenhouse, the greenhouse can be satisfactorily run at

Right: This miniature propagator has dimensions of about 13½ in (34 cm) long and 8 in (20 cm) wide.

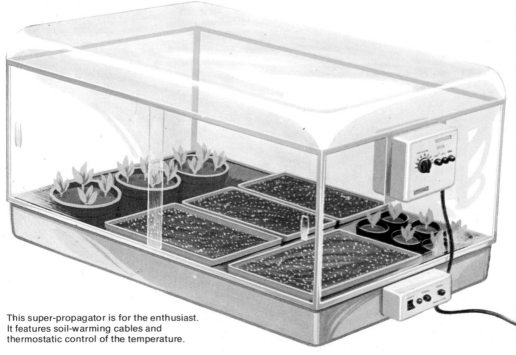

This super-propagator is for the enthusiast. It features soil-warming cables and thermostatic control of the temperature.

10–20°F (5–10°C), lower than it would otherwise be run.

Among the more sophisticated propagation cases that can be purchased, the simplest and smallest consists of a heating panel on which stands a plastic standard seed tray containing sown seeds and covered with a ventilated plastic cover. It can also be used to provide bottom heat for small pot plants and cuttings. They should be stood on *moist* gravel that almost fills the tray. There are more elaborate models, such as a multi-top unit that has four seed trays with covers, and a large one, thermostatically controlled, with greater headroom to allow young plants to grow to maturity. This is, in effect, a miniature heated greenhouse that can be housed in a cooler one.

Above: Mist propagation is useful in rooting cuttings.

Below: By controlling greenhouse lighting, the gardener can make chrysanthemums bloom any time of year that he wishes.

Mist propagation Mention has already been made of the failure to root when a cutting dries off. While it is not a system that many amateurs are likely to employ, mist propagation is one that has been designed to lessen this risk. By this method, cuttings will root better and more quickly.

Fundamentally, the equipment consists of mist nozzles mounted on standpipes and connected to a water-feed pipe, placed at intervals of 3–4 ft (1–1·25 m) along the bench (from which the drainage must be perfect), a control box, a solenoid valve and a detector, which is placed among the cuttings. The latter works on the balance principle and has two arms, one with an absorbent pad, the other being a low-voltage electrical contact. While the cuttings are being sprayed, the pad absorbs moisture and eventually becomes heavy enough to break the electrical contact of the other arm. As moisture evaporates from the pad (and the cuttings get drier), it lightens, contact is made again, and through the solenoid valve and the control box the mist is turned on. This works in conjunction with soil warming.

Greenhouse lighting

For the enthusiast, lighting in the green-house is essential. For general lighting, ordinary light bulbs are quite suitable, however, waterproof fittings are essential.

Another interesting aspect of greenhouse lighting is its use in extending the duration of daylight. Chrysanthemums, in particular, respond to this, because in natural conditions they form their buds during the long summer days, and flower when they shorten. By artificially lengthening and shortening the day by means of lighting, they can be made to bloom at any time.

7 Greenhouse culture

Fertilizing greenhouse plants

Greenhouse plants, like outdoor ones, need certain plant foods. The main ones are nitrogen, potassium, phosphorus, magnesium and a small number of others known as trace elements, in which iron and manganese are normally included, that are consumed in small quantities.

The functions of the main plant foods are as follows.

Nitrogen This element assists in leaf production, but an excess of nitrogen leads to lush growth, prone to disease. It is also an important ingredient in the synthesis of many essential plant chemicals.

Potassium This plays an important role in the plant's manufacture and utilization of starch. It also assists in the development of roots, tubers, seeds and flowers, particularly enhancing the color, and helps to ripen young wood, reducing its vulnerability to disease and early frosts.

Phosphorus This element plays a very important role in the formation of tissue cells and in plant growth. Without it, plants will become stunted.

Magnesium, iron, manganese These three are either essential ingredients of, or essential to the production of chlorophyl, which enables plants to manufacture starch.

Greenhouse plants get their essential foods in the same way as outdoor plants – from fertilizer. The main sources of fertilizers are the composts that are used for potting, which normally contain balanced mixtures. Others are the liquid manures that are subsequently applied.

Composts

Two growing media are used in home greenhouses: the traditional potting composts, and the newer soilless composts, which have to a large extent superseded the former. Though most gardeners now buy their composts, it is as well to know how they are made up.

Potting soils These can vary in the proportion of their major ingredients and added fertilizer materials, but basically contain 2 parts of garden top soil, 1 part peat moss, leafmold or compost, and 1 part coarse sand. For a porous mixture, the peat moss or other organic materials can be

Useful data for greenhouse gardeners:

1 bushel (32 liters) of potting compost is sufficient for:

6 standard seed boxes, 3 in (7·5 cm) deep

90 rooted cuttings in 3 in (7·5 cm) pots

50 larger plants in 4½ in (11·25 cm) pots

16 mature plants in 8 in (20 cm) pots

reduced, eliminated, or increased to reach an especially rich, organic mixture. The fertilizers can be dehydrated manure (easily obtained in bags from garden centers), bone meal or superphosphate. Limestone is added when tests indicate its need.

Soilless Mixes These mixes have great advantages for the home greenhouse owner, one of the first being that the mixes are sterilized. There are several kinds on the market now which differ from each other in slight aspects, but the major ingredients are peat moss, perlite, vermiculite, sand and sufficient fertilizer for about six weeks, after which the grower must start applying liquid foods. Some brands have special formulation for seeds or cuttings or types of plants. Some trade names are Redi-Earth, Pro-Mix, Jiffy Mix.

Propagation

There are a number of ways in which to propagate plants. It must, however, be remembered that only with species is it possible to obtain true reproduction by sowing seeds; many cultivars must be propagated vegetatively – for example, by means of cuttings.

Seed propagation Most seeds will germinate readily if given some heat, ideally by placing them in a propagator.

Seeds should be sown thinly and as shallowly as possible in trays, pans or boxes. If they are very fine, mix them with sand for better distribution. Water them and place them in the propagator. Cover them with brown paper to exclude the light and close the transparent dome. As soon as germination takes place, remove the paper and lift the cover to allow the air to circulate.

When the seedlings are large enough to handle, prick them out. Use a cleft stick to lift them, and firm them into prepared holes in moist compost in another box. Shade the seedlings for a short while until they are established. Finally, when large enough, put each in a pot containing compost.

Stem cuttings Different types of stem cuttings are used for propagating softwoods and hardwoods. For softwood plants, nodal cuttings are usually taken. They should be about 2 in (5 cm) long, cut from a shoot and trimmed off with a sharp knife just below a node (leaf joint). The lower leaves should be removed. The prepared cuttings should be inserted in moist cutting compost in a box, or around the edge of a pot, and kept in a moist, warm atmosphere until growth commences – evidence that roots have formed.

When a good root ball is formed, they should be re-potted into larger pots.

Nodal cuttings of hardwood plants are taken and prepared in much the same way, usually at the end of the growing season. They are usually about 10 in (25 cm) long. They should be inserted into moist compost, and should initially be shaded. When they are growing they should be potted on.

Another type of cutting, often taken from

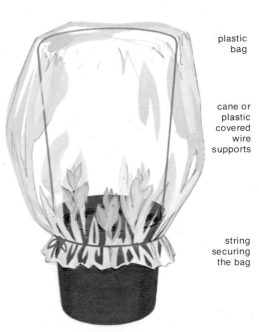

plastic bag

cane or plastic covered wire supports

string securing the bag

An improvised propagator will provide a moist, warm atmosphere for a small number of cuttings.

plants that are more difficult to root, consists of side shoots, of about the same length, torn away from the stem with a heel of the more mature wood. This end should be inserted in moist compost and then be allowed to root.

Stem sections Certain plants, such as ficus and dracaena, can be propagated by cutting a thin section of a stem containing a

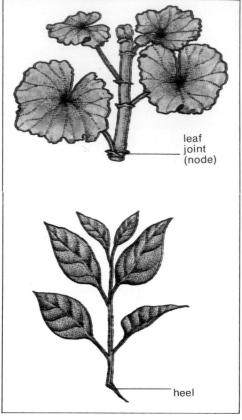

leaf
joint
(node)

heel

bud. When planted just below the surface in cutting compost a good plant will develop.

Leaf-bud cuttings This form of propagation is especially suited to aphelandra, pilea, ficus and camellia. A centrally situated dormant bud is cut out from a semi-ripe wood stem, with a leaf intact. The length of the portion of stem removed should be about ¾ in (2 cm) long. This is planted in a vertical position in cutting compost, with the leaf and bud just above the soil surface.

Division and root cuttings Some plants can be propagated by division. This means that the root of an established plant is cut into several viable portions with a sharp

Above left: A bud cutting. The drawing on the left shows the bud being taken, and on the right planted.

Top: A nodal cutting of a softwood plant
Above: A heel cutting of a hardwood plant

Below: Crocks at the bottom of a seed box will ensure that the box has good drainage.

seed compost

crocks

24

cut

cut

Above: Propagate fleshy-leaved plants by snipping main veins and laying their leaves flat on compost.

Below: Streptocarpus are propagated by dividing a leaf and planting each part upright in compost to root.

knife, and planted in compost. In every case the portion used should have at least one healthy eye or shoot and some healthy roots. This form of propagation can be practiced with chlorophytum, maranta, iris and dahlia. There is also another form of division, applicable to bulbs and corms. These have attached to them smaller bulbs and corms, known as offsets, which can be detached and planted in pots.

Allied to division are root cuttings. These are sections of roots cut into pieces, some 2–3 in (5–7·5 cm) long. They are inserted into compost in boxes.

Air Layering   When some plants (such as the rubber plant) are too high for their surroundings, roots can be made to grow in the stem about 18 in (45 cm) from the top by making a slanting upwards cut three-quarters through the stem. Wedge a small piece of wood into the cut and pack damp peat or moss into the cut around the wound. Wrap polyethylene around the moss and tie it to the stem. After a month, roots will have formed and the rooted part can be cut off and potted up.

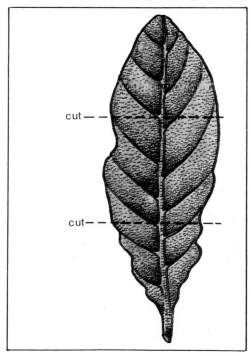

cut

cut

8 Growing vegetables under glass

The range of vegetables that can be grown under glass is somewhat limited, but in many areas of the U.S., mild weather during late fall and winter can allow the hobby greenhouse owner to try out-of-season and exotic varieties.

A greenhouse is also a great asset to a gardener who grows his vegetables outdoors, because it enables him to grow those seedlings which need some heat to germinate, such as celery.

Vegetables can be grown in pots placed on benches, hanging baskets suspended from the roof or in the soil, if the floor is not paved. Even if paving is present, raised beds can be constructed on either side of a narrow walkway.

Individual greenhouse vegetables

Eggplant This delicious and unusual vegetable, expensive to buy, is well worth growing.

Seeds of this annual are sown in an all purpose planting mix and grown at a temperature of 65 degrees F., preferably in a bed warmed by a cable heater, or being placed above tubular heaters. When the seedlings have developed two leaves, trans-plant them into 3 in. pots and later 8 in. pots, using potting soil.

Place them in a warm sunny position. To discourage red spider, spray them twice daily with water. When the plants are 2 ft. tall, pinch out their tips and stop all side shoots two leaves ahead of the fruit.

After they have flowered, encourage the fruit to set by feeding weekly with a liquid fertilizer. Keep the number of fruits down to five per plant. Harvest when the fruits are fully colored.

Good varieties to grow are Dusky and Slim Jim, a producer of small fruit, but excellent performer in pots.

Lettuce Lettuce is best grown in a border on the greenhouse floor, because light requirements are not that critical. Soil should be enriched with organic matter and fertilizer, then raked to a fine tilth. Sow the seeds successively from September to January in three-week intervals for crops from November to spring. Maintain a minimum

Top left: String beans can be grown very successfully and provide very early pickings.

Below: Eggplant does well in a greenhouse, producing nutritious, purple or satiny fruits.

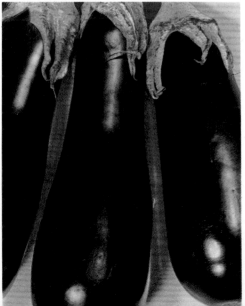

night temperature of 45 degrees F. The use of pelleted seeds is advantageous. Ultimately, thin them out to 9 in. apart. Keep the soil moist, without wetting the leaves, and pay attention to ventilation so that the leaves are not scorched on sunny days. Keep a watchful eye for insects, particularly flies.

Varieties to try are Black-Seeded Simpson, Buttercrunch, Great Lakes and Parris Island Cos.

String Beans These can be successfully grown in pots or in the ground by sowing successively in October, January and February. The required temperature levels are 55 degrees F. by day and 40 degrees F. at night.

For plantings in the ground, start in peat pots, then transplant later.

If growing beans in pots, half-fill an 8 in. pot with moist planting mix and sow seven seeds 1 in. deep. When they are large enough, reduce the number of seedlings to four. Gradually fill the pots with potting soil to 1 in. below the top. Commence watering. As they grow, support the vine with a stake.

As the flowers begin to set, spray them daily with water—this also discourages red spider and thrips—and feed weekly with a liquid fertilizer.

Good varieties to grow are Green Pod, Harvester and Tenderbest.

Rhubarb Early rhubarb can be forced in a greenhouse, but is necessary to do so in complete darkness. This can be done by dividing off a space under the bench, using black plastic sheeting to close off each side. If the bench is slatted, or open, the sheeting will be necessary to close out remaining light. A heat absorbing material should be used to wrap heat pipes, so soil does not dry out.

Left: Lettuce grown on the greenhouse floor provides salads throughout winter.
Below: You can force rhubarb for a winter crop.

Tomatoes are successful greenhouse crops.

First sowings are best made in January and February in pans or seed boxes, with the seeds spaced 1.5 in. apart. The soil medium should be an all-purpose planting mix. Initially, the temperature should be 70 degrees F., then dropped to 60 degrees F. after seven days.

When the seedlings are large enough to handle, healthy specimens should be planted singly in 3 in. pots, watered and shaded for a few days. Once they are 10 in. tall, they should be transplanted permanently into large pots filled with potting soil, or to the planting area on the greenhouse floor. The latter needs advance preparation, by working the soil with a spade or fork, incorporating manure or compost, then watering deeply. Some time after digging, spread 4 oz. of lime per square yard over the surface. At the time of planting fish meal can be worked into the soil. Place seedlings in this bed 18 in. apart.

After transplanting, spray the plants with water twice daily for a short time. Do not saturate the roots. The plants must also be staked. As tomatoes grow, pinch out any shoots as they appear in the leaf axils. Assist pollination by spraying the plants with cold water each bright morning and again in the afternoon during hot weather. This makes

Lift dormant crowns from the garden, place them in the plastic sheeted recess on the ground or flooring, partially cover with soil, then water well. Spray lightly each day. To begin, the temperature should be 45 degrees F., then increased to 50 degrees F. in a week or ten days. Stalks can be harvested when long enough.

One of the best varieties for forcing is Canada Red.

Tomatoes Tomatoes are grown either on the floor in a rich organic soil mix or in pots standing on greenhouse benches. Floor culture is not recommended if glass or glazed greenhouse panels do not extend to the foundation or sill.

All axil shoots of tomatoes should be removed as soon as they are large enough to handle.

Pickling and slicing cucumbers perform well under glass.

come too tall, pinch out the top of the plants.

Well-known commercial greenhouse varieties include Michigan-Ohio Hybrid, Super Fantastic VFN, and Tuckcross 533.

Cucumbers Cucumbers are best sown from February onward, according to the variety, in 3 in. pots filled with a general planting mix — putting one seed in each, pressed in on its side. Maintained at a temperature of 60-65 degrees F., the most robust ones, which will be growing well, will have germinated in about two days. Spray the seedlings with water and keep them shaded. When the root ball is formed, move the sturdy plants into larger pots to give their roots freedom, then throw out the weaklings. As plants grow, support stems with stakes.

In the meantime, prepare a ridge of planting soil, mixed with compost 1 ft. high either along the ground or on the bench. To the above mixture add lime.

When the bed has warmed up, plant your started cucumbers firmly along the top of the ridge 2 ft. apart. Shade the plants from sun and maintain a temperature of 60-65 degrees F.

The atmosphere must be kept humid. Spray the plants twice a day, including soil. Ventilate constantly to provide good air circulation.

Stakes can be used to support the plants, although you may wish to use wire, stretched horizontally across the bed. As plants grow, additional wires can be placed at 8 in. intervals as support.

When roots appear out of the ridge, plants should be top dressed with a mixture of soil and compost. Liquid fertilizer should also be applied. Male flowers must be removed at regular intervals.

A number of slicing and pickling varieties can be adapted for greenhouse culture.

a suitable environment for efficient pollination.

Water daily as the plants grow. Some shading from direct sun on hot days will be beneficial. Shading also helps to keep the temperature steady, although ample ventilation must be provided.

Top-dress pot plants with compost after the second truss has formed. Feed regularly with a liquid fertilizer, commencing with the setting of first fruit. If your tomatoes be-

9 Growing fruit under glass

A greenhouse lends itself very satisfactorily to growing both out-of-season fruit and some of the more exotic varieties that will not stand climatic conditions outdoors.

With a comparatively large greenhouse it is possible to obtain early fruit by planting both tree fruit (for example, apples and pears) and small fruit (for example, raspberries and currants) in large pots and allowing them to stand outdoors for the greater part of the year. They can be brought into shelter during winter months.

Following is a selection of fruits that are well within the scope of the amateur gardener with a relatively small greenhouse.

Individual greenhouse fruits

Apricots This fruit is best grown as a fan-shaped tree, trained on wires standing about 8 in. from the wall of a lean-to or three quarter span greenhouse. The soil in the border should be prepared by digging deeply and incorporating some manure or compost along with some lime. Because apricots cannot stand to have waterlogged roots, make certain soil drains well.

Apricots require a cool greenhouse, with a night temperature not exceeding 45 degrees F. in the early stages, increasing somewhat after stones have formed. Good ventilation should be maintained.

Spray the foliage and soil with water during sunny days to maintain humidity—this also combats red spider. Cease spraying the leaves while the flowers are out and fruits are ripening, but keep the soil damp. As fruits swell, the tree should be given liquid fertilizer applications.

Apricots are pruned mainly by pinching out the young growth in the summer to induce the formation of fruiting spurs and determining the extension growth in the summer. Remove any unwanted wood in the autumn.

Apricots produce reliable crops outdoors where there is plenty of sunshine and in mild locales. Elsewhere, they are best grown in a greenhouse.

A good greenhouse variety of apricot is 'Moorpark.'

Peaches Peaches are similarly grown as fan-trained trees against the wall, in soil prepared the same way as for apricots.

They are mainly cultivated in the same way as apricots. It is necessary, however, to hand-pollinate the flowers using a camel-hair brush. When the fruits are about the size of a hazel nut, they should be thinned to a distance of about 9 in. apart.

The recommended day temperature from flowering to stoning is 45 degrees F. This temperature is progressively increased to 50-65 degrees F. during swelling and ripening then increased again, up to 75 degrees F. to finish the ripening process. During the growing and ripening period, night temperatures should be about 5 degrees lower than daytime.

A number of dwarf short season varieties are available. Dwarfs are recommended because of limited growing space in most hobby greenhouses.

Strawberries

Few greenhouse owners can resist the temptation of early strawberries, which can be readily grown in pots on the bench.

Healthy plants should be planted during June and July in 3 in. pots containing an all-purpose potting soil. The pots should be placed in the garden until October, when plants should be repotted into 6 in. pots and kept in a cold frame. In November or December, they should be brought inside. The starting temperature should be 50 degrees F., rising to 60 degrees F. with the night temperature no more than 50 degrees F. as they come into flower. During this period, the humidity should be kept high, by spraying the plants on bright days.

Do not water lavishly at first. When flowers begin to appear, water well, and feed weekly with liquid fertilizer until the fruits begin to color. It is advisable to hand-pollinate with a camel hair brush because air flow is largely cut off and few insects are available to transmit pollen naturally. Do not allow more than eight flowers to form fruit. Ventilate well, but avoid cold drafts. After flowering, increase the temperature somewhat.

In areas with mild winters, a second batch can be brought in from the frame in January to provide a second crop.

There are many good strawberry varieties available. It is a good idea, however, to select one that will fit into your outdoor gardening program.

Above: Peaches respond well to being grown in a greenhouse and are more reliable there than when they are grown out-of-doors in many areas.

Below: Early strawberries grown in pots give a gourmet touch to spring meals.

Many grape varieties will grow well in an unheated greenhouse where winters are mild, producing large clusters, such as above and right.

Grapes There is little doubt that grapes are the most delicious fruit that can be grown without difficulty in a greenhouse. One point that bothers many amateurs who wish to grow grapes under glass is the possibility that the fully developed vine may take away light from other plants. This worry, however, can be overcome by training the growing shoots across the north gable. In mild areas, some gardeners plant the vine outside and train stems through an aperture into the interior. Grapevines are also suitable for training on the wall of a lean-to style or three-quarter-span greenhouse.

The vine should be planted in well-drained deeply dug soil to which well-rotted manure or garden compost has been added. Top dress with lime or bonemeal. If more than one vine is being planted, space them 3-4 feet apart. The soil and atmosphere in the greenhouse should be kept

32

moist. Some ventilation should also be provided. The amount of heating needed will vary by area. In some parts of the U.S. grapes require little or no heat. There are, however, a few varieties, such as the Muscats that need a long growing season and do best at a temperature of 50-55 degrees F.

It is important for grapes not to be exposed to cold drafts or dryness during the short time when they are about the size of a currant (the stoning period). When they begin to swell again, the number of clusters should be thinned, using a pruning shears or vine scissors.

Training and pruning a vine are important factors in its culture. The growing shoots should be trained along horizontal wires fixed at intervals on the structure, set 1 ft. apart and 6 in. from the glass.

The pruning program is as follows. In the first winter, train the leading shoot as far up as possible. Cut back all laterals when they have become 2 ft. long. In the second winter, prune the main leader back by half or back to old wood. Cut laterals to one or two buds.

During subsequent springs, on shooting, select the best growth from each fruiting spur and rub out the rest. As these shoots grow, stop them two leaves beyond the flowers. Stop all sub-laterals (the side shoots on these shoots) at one leaf along their length.

Allow fruiting to develop slowly. Remove all bunches in the first year. Allow only a few to develop in the second year after planting. An increasing number of clusters can be left on in succeeding years.

Melons

Among the many delicious fruits that can be easily grown in the greenhouse, melons can be produced at a time when they are expensive to buy.

Plants can be raised from seeds to crop from May onwards by successive sowing at monthly intervals from January to May. Seeds are planted 1/2 in. deep, edgeways in 3 in. pots. The seeds are germinated at a temperature of 64 degrees F. The temperature is then increased to 61 degrees F. and pots are set near the glass. Once plants can be handled easily, replant into 5 in. pots.

When the plants have reached their fifth leaf, transplant them to a bed prepared around the inside perimeter of the greenhouse. This bed should contain well-prepared soil enriched with well-rotted manure or garden compost. Where a paved floor is present, the plants can be grown-on in 9 in. pots. Each plant should have a stake inserted alongside it, to which it can be trained until it reaches the horizontal wires erected as described under 'Cucumbers' on page 29.

When the main stem has reached the top wire, the growing tip is pinched out, and the laterals are similarly reduced when they reach five leaves long. The flowers, male and female, develop on the sub-laterals.

During early growth, maintain good humidity by dampening the soil around the plants and spraying the leaves until fruits reach their full size. Shade from sun, but otherwise give the plants maximum light. Artificially pollinate, preferably at midday, by removing petals from the male flower and inserting centers of each one into female flowers.

Keep the number of fruits down to four per plant, and not more than one to a sub-lateral.

When the fruits are about 2 3/4 in. in diameter feed with a liquid fertilizer weekly and water well every morning with lukewarm water until they are fully grown. Because of their weight, melons should be supported in nets attached to the wires.

Both honeydew and cantaloupe melons do well under glass. A number of high producing varieties are available.

Cantaloupe, like those illustrated here, can be successfully grown in a greenhouse. Started plants can be grown on in pots or in a bed prepared on the greenhouse floor.

10 Growing plants under glass

At the beginning of each of the descriptions that follow is a recommendation pertaining to the type of greenhouse needed for successful cultivation of the plant in question. Sometimes alternatives are suggested: for example, 'cool or warm'. Generally, while a specific plant can be grown under the cooler conditions, it is normally better when cultivated at the higher temperature.

Anthurium scherzerianum
(flamingo plant, painter's palette)
Tropical or warm. A most colorful plant with a bold, bright scarlet, wax-like spathe about 3 in (7·5 cm) wide and long, enclosing a spiral orange-red spike (spadix). Its leaves are long, shiny, lance-shaped and light green.

It is propagated by dividing the rootstock in February. The divisions are planted in potting compost in such a way that the roots are high in the pot on a slight mound. Half-fill the pot, which should be 6 in (15 cm) across if the size warrants it, with crocks. This plant needs humidity.

Anthurium scherzerianum is a colorful, fascinating and very exotic plant.

Aphelandra squarrosa 'Louisae' (zebra plant)
Tropical or warm. A very popular, beautiful, showy plant. It has 10 in (25 cm) long pointed dark green leaves with veins that are boldly cream in color. During summer and autumn it produces yellow flowers, which should be removed as they fade. Two other attractive varieties are *A. squarrosa* 'Brockfield' and *A. squarrosa* 'Silver Beauty'.

Aphelandra are propagated from cuttings taken during the spring and summer and rooted in sowing compost at 70°F (21°C) in a propagator. They should be potted on in potting compost. Feed while they are in flower.

Aspidistra elatior
(cast-iron plant, parlor palm)
Cool. This foliage plant was a great favorite of the Victorians and Edwardians. It has beautiful long, wide, shiny green leaves.

Aphelandra squarrosa is beautiful but difficult to grow.

A. *elatior* 'Variegata' has cream variegated leaves.

This plant needs little attention, although it is beneficial to sponge its leaves from time to time. It is best to re-pot it in the spring, but this should be carried out only after several years.

Propagate by dividing the rhizome in March so that each piece has some leaf and roots. Plant in potting compost.

Begonia

Cool or warm. *Begonia rex* is grown entirely for the beauty of its leaves, which include silver, dark green, pink and darkest purple colours. It is propagated by means of the leaves, which are cut across the back of the main veins and pinned down flat on a surface of cutting compost in a tray. They are then placed in a propagator at 64–70°F (18–21°C). Another interesting foliage begonia is *B. masoniana* (iron cross begonia).

B. semperflorens is fibrous-rooted and has red, pink or white flowers; these begonias make lovely greenhouse plants for the later autumn. Seeds are sown in late June. They should be put into a propagator at 64°F (18°C) and then potted on. They like humid conditions.

Begonia 'Gloire de Lorraine' (Christmas begonia) is winter-flowering, with clusters

Aspidistra elatior 'Variegata' is grown for its foliage.

of delicate rose-pink flowers. It is propagated from cuttings and basal shoots taken in spring and ultimately potted on in 6 in (15 cm) pots. It likes a moist and semi-shady warm position when potted. Its stems must be supported. Remove all flower buds until October, when they should be allowed to develop, and then give weekly doses of liquid fertilizer. After flowering, cut the plants down by half and keep them, watering little, until early spring at which time they will provide more cuttings.

Beloperone guttata (shrimp plant)

Warm. This plant's common name results from its pinkish-brown bracts that resemble shrimps. It prefers a warm house and should be grown in well-drained potting compost. It should be given plenty of water during the summer, but little in the winter.

Cuttings should be taken in early summer and inserted in soilless sowing compost

Few greenhouse plants are more beautiful than *Begonia rex*, with its colorful, almost triangular leaves.

Beloperone guttata has become a favorite exotic pot plant. It seldom exceeds 1 ft (30 cm) in height.

at 64°F (18°C), and then potted on into 3 in (7·5 cm) pots and afterwards 5 in (13 cm) pots. Bushiness should be induced by regular pinching back of the shoots. When established, give liquid manure regularly during the summer.

Bouvardia longiflora (syn. humboldtii) (Sweet Bouvardia)

Warm or cool. Nowadays it is usual to grow varieties, of which 'President Cleveland', with its terminal clusters of bright crimson-scarlet tubular flowers, is representative. They flower from fall through winter.

After flowering, rest the plants with little watering until late spring. Then water the soil and spray the stems to start fresh growth. Also prune, if necessary. Pinch back during the summer to encourage late flowering.

Propagate from cuttings from young shoots placed in a propagator at 66°F (19°C), or from root cuttings.

Brunfelsia (syn. Franciscea) calycina

Tropical or warm. Has fragrant, salvia-shaped violet-purple flowers with a long tube, which fade to almost white from winter to spring. The variety 'Macrantha' has 3 in (7·5 cm) wide flowers.

After flowering, shorten the stalks by half and encourage new growth by spraying with water. Provide a moist atmosphere.

Propagate from cuttings taken between February and August. Insert in soilless cutting compost and give bottom heat at about 70°F (21°C).

Bulbs
(spring)

Most bulbs are easy to grow, and do not need any great heat. They provide a magnificent display in the greenhouse. A few planted successively from late summer onwards will bloom from Christmas until

May. As they spend much of their growing time in plunge beds outdoors, they do not take up space in the greenhouse for long.

The most popular bulbs are daffodils, hyacinths and tulips. Daffodils and hyacinths should be planted so that their noses are just visible through the surface of the soil, tulips should be just covered, and small bulbs such as crocuses and snow-drops buried by ¼–½ in (6–12 mm).

The following description of the cultivation of daffodil bulbs is fairly typical, despite small modifications for other bulbs.

Daffodil bulbs should be planted in a general purpose soil mixture or a soilless potting mixture. A 6 in (15 cm) pot will accommodate three or four bulbs.

After planting, place the pot in the soil in a cool plunge bed outdoors for about eight weeks, when the young, pale green leaves appear. Then bring them into the green-

house and stand them in a dim light until the leaves turn green, when the pot should be given more light and warmth – a day temperature of 50°F (10°C) – until the plants flower. Water as necessary.

After they have flowered, put the pots outside. When the leaves are dead, harvest and dry the bulbs, and plant them *outdoors* the following fall.

Daffodil bulbs which are planted in August–October will flower from early to late winter, according to variety and when the plants are brought into the greenhouse.

Tulip bulbs planted in September–October flower from January to April. These will stand rather more heat, up to 60°F (15°C).

Hyacinth bulbs planted in September–October flower from January to March. These usually take about seven weeks to produce growth when plunged.

Trumpet daffodils brighten the dark days of winter.

Calceolaria are best grown in pots under glass.

Calceolaria
(slipper flower)
Cool. It is the herbaceous calceolaria that is grown most frequently in a greenhouse. This has large clusters of red-orange and red flowers with distinctive markings and ovate mid-green leaves. Many fine hybrids are obtainable.

The seeds are sown thinly in seed compost and germinated at 64°F (18°C) during June, with shading when needed. Prick off the seedlings singly into pots in July and keep in a cold frame. In September pot on into 4 in (10 cm) pots and take inside. Keep warm and moist at night at a steady temperature. In February pot on again in 8 in (20 cm) pots using growing compost. Keep near the glass, shading from strong sun. Stake securely and water modestly. Feed with liquid manure fortnightly when buds appear.

Camellia

Cool. These popular plants are much appreciated for their shapely white, pink and red flowers and their rich green, shiny, bold foliage. They need comparatively little attention other than regular, fairly modest watering and occasional feeding. They might need re-potting every three or four years.

They can be propagated by taking leaf bud cuttings.

Campanula isophylla
(Italian bellflower)

Cool. *Campanula isophylla* is a prostrate plant, which overhangs the rim of its pot and has star-shaped blue flowers in abundance during August and September. Its cultivar *Campanula isophylla* 'Alba', with white blooms, is even more charming. It is useful for hanging baskets.

It should be watered and fed regularly while flowering and dead-headed regularly. Do not overwater in winter.

Propagate from cuttings from sturdy basal shoots taken in spring. Insert these in cutting compost and provide some warmth.

Carnations

Cool. Carnations will produce flowers continuously throughout the year, with some peak periods, in a cool, well-ventilated greenhouse with plenty of headroom.

New carnations are usually supplied in spring in 3 in (7·5 cm) pots. On arrival they

Campanula isophylla 'Alba' is excellent for using in a hanging basket.

can be transplanted into 6 in (15 cm) pots, or to a raised 9 in (22·5 cm) high bed on the ground, of a rich organic soil that is slightly alkaline. Place the plants 8 in (20 cm) apart each way in the bed.

When the plants are growing well, pinch their tips out to encourage the growth of side-shoots. When these are about 6 in (15 cm) long, they in turn can have all the buds removed, except one, so that each stem only bears one good bloom.

Regular watering is very important: water quite copiously during the summer, with much less in winter when growth slows up. A night temperature of up to 50°F (10°C) is suitable; during the summer a little light shading might be needed to lower the daytime temperature.

Carnations should be supported with canes and wire rings when in pots, and with large-mesh netting, about 6 in (15 cm), strung from four corner posts when growing in a bed. After the first blooms are cut, the carnations should then be fed with a fertilizer which is suitable for carnations.

Carnations last two years, so new stocks should be raised by taking side cuttings in early spring. Plant them in cutting compost and place them in a propagator at 61–64°F (16–18°C), admitting air when the tips begin to grow and lowering the temperature to 50°F (10°C) over the course of a week. Then pot into 3 in (7·5 cm) pots. When they are 9 in (22·5 cm) tall, remove the growing tip; repeat if desired when the resultant side shoots are long enough. Pot on when needed.

Chlorophytum (spider plant)

Cool or warm. *Chlorophytum elatum* 'Variegatum' is the variety most grown, solely for its long, grass-like leaves, which are green with a broad streak of white running down their center. These plants are excellent for hanging baskets.

The spider plant is very easy to grow. Apart from reasonable watering during the summer, and a regular feed with liquid manure, little more is needed.

Inconspicuous flowers develop in the ends of long slender stems, weighing them down. Chlorophytum can be propagated by planting the plantlets that are formed as the flowers fade. Otherwise, root divisions can be taken in spring or summer.

Chrysanthemum (late-flowering)

Cool. Start with disease-free, rooted cuttings. Subsequently new plants can be raised by taking cuttings from the old plants.

To do this, cut selected healthy plants down to 6–9 in (15–22·5 cm) *immediately* after flowering, still keeping them in their pots. Give an initial watering, and keep

them in a light airy position in the greenhouse at a temperature no higher than 50°F (10°C) without much further watering.

After a time basal shoots will appear. Choose healthy shoots about ⅛ in (3 mm) thick, with four or five fresh leaves closely spaced along the stem, for cuttings. Guard

Chlorophytum elatum 'Variegatum' (spider plant) is very easy to grow and propagate.

against aphids by spraying them with malathion. Propagate by cutting the shoots just below a node.

If necessary, trim off any lower leaves to facilitate planting. Wet the lower ends of the stems and insert in a rooting compound. Shake off the surplus powder, and insert in coarse sand and peat moss or soil-less cutting compost, 2 in (5 cm) apart, in a seed-box. Place the cuttings in a moist atmosphere and provide bottom heat up to about 60°F (15°C) for about a week or ten days, preferably in a propagator. When they show signs of growth shade them with paper on bright days, and when they become robust give the cuttings both ventilation and a temperature which is no higher than 45°F (7°C).

When they are well rooted, transplant the cuttings into a general purpose potting soil or soilless potting compost in 3 in (7·5 cm) pots and place them in a cold frame. About the end of May, when the root ball is well-formed, move into 9 in (22·5 cm) pots. At the same time, insert two stakes, at least 3 ft (1 m) tall, in the compost either side of the plant. Tie each stem securely but not tightly to these.

Stand the potted chrysanthemums outdoors in rows on boards or another hard surface for the summer. To prevent them from blowing over, tie the stakes to horizontal wires running along the rows. In late September bring the pots into the greenhouse, giving them good ventilation and a little heat.

Chrysanthemums first form a terminal bud on the main stem. As soon as the side shoots appear at the leaf joints, remove this bud, for it will either die or give poor flowers. Allow the side shoots to develop buds. The center large one, known as the first crown bud, produces the best decorative blooms. All the other buds on each side shoot that is retained should be removed, leaving one bloom to a stem. All further

Clivia miniata blooms best when it is pot-bound. It is as tough and durable as the aspidistra.

side shoots should also be pinched out as they form.

Clivia miniata

Cool. This plant has strap-shaped leaves and lily-like clusters of flowers of orange-red. Young plants need re-potting every

Chrysanthemums are first 'stopped' by pinching out the 'break bud', which either dies or flowers poorly, appearing on the main stem when shoots first appear in the leaf axils (*left*). The latter are eventually 'disbudded' to leave the center bud or 'first crown bud', which usually produces the best blooms. It is then 'secured' by removing any further axil shoots that appear (*right*).

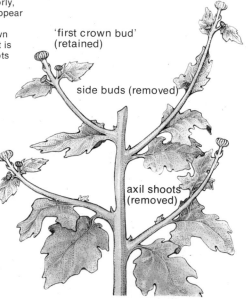

'first crown bud' (retained)

'break bud' (pinch out)

side buds (removed)

axil shoots (removed)

main stem

side (axil) shoots

40

year into 8 in (20 cm) pots. Mature plants may remain undisturbed for several years if they are top-dressed with fresh rich soil annually, and fed occasionally with liquid manure. After they have flowered keep them warm and moist. Then give them a resting period, which can be induced by minimizing watering.

Propagation is best achieved by division after flowering or from offsets.

Codiaeum
(croton)

Tropical or warm. Various crotons are grown for their leaves, variegated with brilliant hues ranging from yellow to orange-pink, red and crimson. These colors are more vivid in plants raised annually.

The plants need a moist, very warm atmosphere all the time and must have good light. They should be well watered during the summer and given a weekly feed of liquid fertilizer. They are best potted on annually in spring.

They can be propagated by cuttings at any time from the ends of shoots, inserted singly in 2 in (5 cm) pots of cutting compost and put into a propagator at 70°F (21°C).

Good crotons to grow are *Codiaeum variegatum pictum* and its cultivars 'Duke of Windsor,' 'Elaine' and 'Imperialis'.

Coleus blumei

Cool or warm. Coleus are grown for their colorful foliage. They should be regularly watered during the summer, and much less so in winter. A temperature of 55°F (13°C) is best in winter. Feed with liquid manure weekly from June to September. Growing tips should be pinched.

Codiaeum variegatum pictum (croton) is extremely rewarding but is not really easy to grow.

Seeds may be sown in February and germinated at 61°F (16°C). When large enough, pot the seedlings on into 3 in (7·5 cm) and then 5 in (13 cm) pots. Alternatively, take tip cuttings of non-flowering shoots in spring. Plant them in cutting compost in 3 in (7·5 cm) pots and keep them in a temperature of 61–64°F (16–18°C).

Columnea gloriosa is a beautiful trailer. Though not the easiest to grow, it is well worth persevering with it.

Columnea gloriosa

Warm. With its tubular flowers of bright scarlet and drooping habit, *Columnea gloriosa* is ideal for hanging baskets. It flowers during the winter.

It needs a warm, humid atmosphere (no lower than 55–61°F (13–16°C) during winter). Feed established plants regularly with weak liquid manure during the summer. Re-pot this plant every other year in June.

Pieces of stems root quite easily in a cutting compost placed in a propagator with a temperature of 64–70°F (18–21°C) and a humid atmosphere. The stem pieces should be taken in spring.

Cyclamen persicum

Cool or warm. The modern strains of the Persian cyclamen, a popular winter-flowering plant, have blooms in shades of purple, red, pink, mauve and white and combinations of these, and variously silver-marbled leaves.

The plants should be brought into the greenhouse in September and given ample ventilation, light and a temperature of 50°F (10°C). Watering must be done carefully from the bottom without wetting the bare corms. After flowering, the plants should be rested by gradually watering less and, during the summer, laying the pots on their sides to dry off. In autumn, growth should be re-started by watering.

Cyclamen are best propagated from seeds sown in August at a temperature of 55–61°F (13–16°C). Then pot them on until they are in 5 in (13 cm) pots. At no stage should the corms be buried.

Dieffenbachia picta
(dumb cane)

Warm. This has dark green, pointed, oblong leaves covered with white and pale green spots. Its cultivar 'Rudolph Roehrsii' is mottled pale and dark green.

Dieffenbachia needs a humid atmosphere with a winter temperature not lower than 61°F (16°C).

It is propagated from suckers or stem sections containing an eye in a cutting compost at a temperature of 70–75°F (21–24°C) in a propagator.

Dracaena draco
(dragon plant)

The species and varieties of dracaenas are grown for their superb range of foliage. Among the more attractive species are the smaller *Dracaena godseffiana* and *D. sanderiana*. A large cultivar is *D. deremensis* 'Warneckii', which has long gray-green leaves with two silver stripes. *D. draco*, the dragon tree, is a unique tree with a tall, heavy trunk and odd tufts of foliage. Young plants are used as pot subjects.

Dracaena fragrans 'Massangena' has attractive green and gold leaves and likes a warm, humid atmosphere.

The plants need a winter temperature of 50–55°F (10–13°C), rising to 61°F (16°C) at night in spring and summer to encourage growth. The atmosphere must be humid.

They are propagated from cuttings of a main stem, partially buried horizontally in cutting compost in a propagator at 70–75°F (21–24°C).

Euphorbia pulcherrima (poinsettia)

Warm or tropical. This splendid plant has insignificant flowers, but large scarlet, leaf-like bracts in winter. It is also available in pink and cream forms. The new hybrids are especially rugged, lasting for months in good condition.

It needs a winter temperature of 55–61°F (13–16°C). During the summer it needs a humid atmosphere. It should be watered freely while growing, but after flowering it should be kept just moist. Give weak liquid manure weekly from June to September, during which period it can stand outdoors.

Poinsettia is difficult to preserve from one season to another so it is better to grow new plants from cuttings taken in spring. These should be inserted singly in 3 in (7·5 cm) pots of cutting compost and placed in a propagator at 64–70°F (18–21°C). The rooted cuttings should be potted on, and feeding should begin in their final pots.

Ficus elastica 'Decora' (India-rubber plant)

Warm. This plant is grown for its rich, green, bold foliage.

In winter it needs a temperature of 61–64°F (16–18°C). Water freely in summer and keep just moist in winter. Place in a well-lit position, but out of direct sunlight. Provide a humid atmosphere in summer, with ventilation when needed,

Few plants can surpass *Euphorbia pulcherrima* (poinsettia) for the splendid color it gives.

There are many beautiful varieties of indoor fuchsia, which are grown as both bushes and standards.

and pot on every other spring. Feed with weak liquid manure during the summer.

The plant can be propagated from cuttings of lateral shoots taken from April to June at a temperature of 70–75°F (21–24°C), or from leaf-bud cuttings.

Fuchsia

Cool or warm. The tender varieties of fuchsia are attractive as pot plants and provide beautiful summer flower displays in greenhouses.

After resting during winter, when they should be kept in a dry, well-lit place at a temperature 39–45°F (4–7°C), fuchsias should be started into growth by being plunged into water and kept at a temperature of 50°F (10°C). (Any cuttings required should be taken when the young growth appears.) After removing as much soil as possible from the roots, pot the plants in a standard potting compost in a similar or smaller pot.

During the spring and summer fuchsias should be allowed to stand in a cool, well-lit place out of direct sunlight. Real success with fuchsias results from feeding and watering well during the growing and flowering season. Spraying the foliage with water occasionally will also prove beneficial to the plant.

Cuttings should be taken from shoots with no flower buds and should be nodal. They should be inserted in 2 in (5 cm) pots of cutting compost and placed in a propagator at 61°F (16°C) until they are rooted, when air should be allowed in and the temperature lowered to 50°F (10°C). Young plants destined to be bushes must have their growing tip pinched back to induce bushiness. This may be repeated once or twice more if necessary. For standards, the plants should not be pinched back, but the main stem should be allowed to grow, removing all laterals as they appear, until the required height is reached, when it should be stopped.

Fuchsia bushes should be pruned lightly in February. At this time, overgrown plants can be hard-pruned to reduce their size. Standards are also pruned.

Pendulous varieties, such as 'Falling Stars' and golden-foliaged 'Golden Marinka', are excellent for hanging baskets, either to beautify a greenhouse, or to hang outdoors during the summer providing a glorious display.

Gerbera
(Transvaal daisy, Barberton daisy)

Cool. *Gerbera jamesonii* has orange-scarlet, daisy-like flowers from May to December. There are also many hybrids and varieties in a wide range of colors.

Gerbera needs well-drained soil and cool conditions, with a temperature of 41–45°F (5–7C) during the winter. Water freely in summer and more sparingly in winter, ventilate well and provide some shade when necessary. Apply weak liquid manure every two weeks during the summer.

Gerbera can be propagated by division in March. Alternatively, sow seeds in seed compost in February at a temperature of 61–64°F (16–18°C). Prick out and pot on in the usual manner.

Above: Grevillea robusta is beautiful and easy-to-grow.

Below right: Hoya carnosa is relatively unknown.

Grevillea robusta
(silk bark oak)

Cool. *Grevillea robusta* is a foliage shrub with pinnate leaves up to 15 in (37·5 cm) long.

It requires a winter temperature of 39–45°F (4–7°C) and can be stood out of doors from May to October. Water freely in spring and summer and keep just moist during winter. Feed fortnightly with liquid manure during summer. Re-pot in March every two years, increasing the pot size if necessary.

This plant is propagated from seed sown in March in pots of lime-free sowing compost and germinated at 55–61°F (13–16°C). Prick out into 3 in (7·5 cm) pots and then pot on as necessary.

Hippeastrum
(amaryllis)

Warm or tropical. Hippeastrum are showy, bulbous plants with strap-like green leaves and blooms of white, pink, red or orange, sometimes striped or frilled, according to the hybrid.

Plant one bulb in a 6 in (15 cm) pot of growing compost with half the bulb exposed and water sparsely until growth begins. As soon as the flower bud appears, or shortly afterwards, water freely and feed weekly with liquid manure. Maintain at a minimum temperature of 55–61°F (13–16°C). When leaves turn yellow, keep dry until re-starting growth in autumn.

Propagate from offsets or seeds sown in the springtime.

Hoya carnosa
(porcelain flower)

Cool or warm. This is a climber with deep green, glossy leaves and clusters of pale pink, sweetly scented flowers during summer.

Keep *H. carnosa* at 50°F (10°C) in winter and at not less than 61°F (16°C) in spring and summer. Provide a little shade when necessary, and abundant water, except in winter. Maintain a good level of humidity in spring and summer and also spray the plant with water when hot. Give liquid manure every three weeks in summer.

The plant is propagated by cuttings 3 in

(7·5 cm) long taken in June and July. Root
at 61–64°F (16–18°C) in a propagator.

Impatiens sultanii
(busy Lizzie)

Cool or warm. Busy Lizzie has white,
orange, magenta, crimson or scarlet flowers
from April to October.

It needs a winter temperature of 55°F
(13°C). When growth re-starts in March,

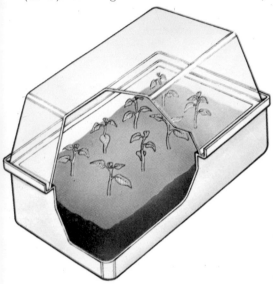

Above: Impatiens sultanii can be propagated from tip
cuttings in a propagating unit given bottom heat.

Right: Maranta leuconeura 'Kerchoveana' is called the
'prayer plant' because it raises its leaves at sundown.

water fairly freely. Liquid-feed weekly from
May to September and provide a little
shade on hot days. Re-pot every other year
in April.

Propagate from tip cuttings inserted in
cutting compost at any time from April to
May. Place in a propagator at 61°F (16°C).

Jasminum mesneyi (syn. primulinum)
and J. polyanthum

Cool. *Jasminum mesneyi* (syn. *primulinum*) has
yellow flowers in spring. *J. polyanthum* has
white and pale pink blooms in winter. Both
are climbers.

Both do best in a greenhouse border, but
they can be grown in 12 in (30 cm) pots.
They should be trained up wires. In winter,
a satisfactory temperature is 50–55°F
(10–13°C). Keep the compost moist continuously and water freely during the growing season.

Propagate from heel cuttings and give
bottom heat of 61°F (16°C).

Maranta

Warm or tropical. Ornamental foliage
plants, with leaves of various shapes
marked or streaked in vivid colors. The two
most strikingly colored plants are *Maranta
leuconeura* 'Kerchoveana' and *M. l.
erythrophylla*.

They need a winter temperature of 55°F

(13°C), ample watering in summer, more
moderate watering in winter, a humid
atmosphere, a daily spraying and a fortnightly liquid feed during their growing
season.

They are propagated by rhizome division in April or by planting basal shoot
cuttings in the summer in cutting compost
at 70°F (21°C).

Above: Howea belmoreana can have a striking decorative effect.

Left: Neanthe elegans is a perfect palm to grow because it requires so little attention.

Palms

Cool. Small palms make good table decorations, and the larger specimens are most attractive for the greenhouse and conservatory. Among the most excellent is *Chamaedorea* (syn. *Neanthe*) *elegans* 'Bella' (parlor palm), with elegant pinnate leaves, up to 4 ft (1·25 m) long, that hang down gracefully. It should be watered freely in summer and have its leaves sprayed weekly. Feed throughout the growing season. Give partial shade: too much sun turns the foliage brown. It needs repotting only when it becomes pot-bound, and this is rare.

Howea (formerly *Kentia*) *belmoreana* (curly palm) is a palm with dark green pinnate leaves 18 in (45 cm) long and 12 in (30 cm) wide, carried on 18 in (45 cm) long stems.

Howea (formerly *Kentia*) *forsteriana* (Ken-

tia palm), another excellent species, has leaves that differ from those of *H. belmoreana* only in that they droop and have fewer leaflets.

Both of these are grown in a growing compost. Ideally, they should be given a winter greenhouse temperature of 50–54°F (10–12°C); the minimum should be 45°F (7°C). *Howea* need full light in winter, with some shading in summer. Water sparingly between November and March, abundantly from April to July and moderately between July and October.

All the above-mentioned palms can be propagated from seed. Place the seed on the surface of some peat in a seed-pan, and germinate at a temperature of 81°F (27°C). Transplant to 3 in (7·5 cm) pots of growing compost and maintain a temperature of 64°F (18°C) until they are growing.

Pelargonium
(Geranium)

Cool or warm. Fuchsias and pelargoniums have a number of common uses, including greenhouse display, hanging baskets, indoor pot plants and summer bedding.

Among the pelargoniums there are two outstanding groups of hybrids – the regal *P. × domesticum*, among which there are some very beautiful varieties, *P. × hortorum*, and the zonal pelargoniums. These latter are commonly known as geraniums, and include hundreds of outstanding named cultivars. There are also varieties of foliage geraniums, both pendulous types and miniature ones which are suitable for hanging baskets.

Although pelargoniums can be maintained in a greenhouse from year to year, it is more common to take cuttings annually.

Nodal cuttings are taken in August and inserted individually in 3 in (7·5 cm) pots of a general purpose mixture, or in soilless sowing compost. Keep them covered with paper from seven to ten days. Normally no heat is required for rooting. Pinch out the growing tips to form good bushes when the plants are about 6 in (15 cm) high. Pot on into 4–6 in (10–15 cm) pots. Maintain a

Above: Pelargoniums are among the most popular and colorful plants to cultivate in a greenhouse.
Left: Zonal pelargoniums are available in many colorful varieties, all of which are most attractive.

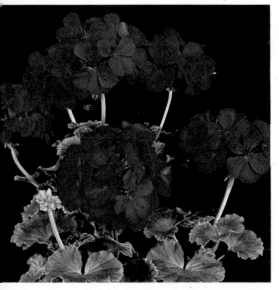

winter temperature of 45–50°F (7–10°C) and keep the soil just moist. Water freely during the growing season. Keep the greenhouse well ventilated and provide shade during the hottest weather – do not let the temperature exceed 55°F (13°C). When well-rooted feed with liquid manure until the flowers open.

Peperomia

Warm or tropical. Mostly moderate-sized or small plants. They like shade from the sun, and grow in well-drained compost. They should have a humid atmosphere during summer and be sprayed twice daily, but they must not be overwatered and be allowed to dry out before the next watering. The best winter temperature for them is 55–65°F (13–18°C) and in summer 60–75°F (15–24°C).

They are propagated by cuttings inserted singly 2 in (5 cm) pots of cutting compost in a propagator at 75°F (24°C).

Pilea

Warm or tropical. The best known are *Pilea cadierei* (aluminum plant) and *P. muscosa* (artillery plant).

They require a winter temperature of 55°F (13°C) and a summer one of 75°F (24°C). They also need full light in winter and moderate shade in spring and summer. Water freely from April to September, very moderately in winter. Feed fortnightly during summer.

Propagate from cuttings in May. Insert in cutting compost and place in the propagator at 64–70°F (18–21°C).

Plumbago capensis

Cool or warm, *Plumbago capensis* is a lovely deciduous climbing plant with panicles of

Peperomia caperata has curious cream flowers, like shepherd's crooks, borne on light brown stalks.

Pilea cadierei is a very charming foliage plant.

blue flowers from April to November.

While it can be grown in a pot, it is best planted in the border and trained up wires or a trellis. It should be watered well until after flowering, and then kept just moist and watered increasingly as new growth appears. The best temperature up to December is 55–61°F (13–16°C); the minimum during the winter is 45°F (7°C). Feed regularly during the summer and re-pot annually in the spring.

Propagate from heel cuttings at a temperature of 61–64°F (16–18°C).

Primula

Cool. Primulas are excellent for greenhouses. Possibly the most popular for growing under glass are *Primula malacoides*, *P. sinensis*, *P. obconica* and *P. ×kewensis*.

P. malacoides, although a perennial, is usually grown as an annual. Its leaves are hairy, ovate and pale green. Whorls of star-like flowers, ranging from pale lilac to white open between December and April.

P. sinensis is also a perennial grown as an annual. Its thick stems bear two or three whorls of flowers during winter.

49

P. obconica is also grown as an annual. Its light green leaves cause a rash on sensitive skins. Its winter-produced flowers are in clusters of pink, red, lilac or blue-purple.

P. ×kewensis, a perennial hybrid, has fragrant, yellow flowers, borne in whorls on upright stems during the winter.

All primulas require a minimum winter temperature 45°F (7°C). Always keep the plant moist. Feed weekly with liquid manure when the flower stalks start to lengthen.

All are propagated from seeds at 61°F (16°C). Prick off the seedlings into boxes, and transplant them singly into 3 in (7·5 cm) pots of growing compost. Plunge

A very beautiful plant, *Primula obconica* must be handled with care, as its leaves affect sensitive skin.

Rhododendron (syn. *Azalea*) *indicum* is a lovely plant for Christmas decoration.

them outdoors in a shaded frame for the summer. In autumn, pot them on to 6 in (15 cm) pots.

Rhododendron (syn. Azalea) indicum (Indoor or Indian azalea)

Cool or warm. This is an evergreen with many hybrids which become massed in red, pink or white flowers during the winter or early spring.

In autumn the plant should be kept in a well-lighted place and sprayed with clear water. The compost should be kept moist, but should not become over-wet.

After it has flowered, remove the dead flowers and put outdoors in the sun after the danger of frost has passed. During the summer keep the plant in the shade, water and feed until early October and then bring it back under the glass. If necessary, re-pot into a larger pot after flowering.

Propagate from half-ripened cuttings taken in April, inserted in cutting compost with a little bottom heat. They are not easy to root. Rooting compounds and mist propagation will be helpful, however.

Saintpaulia (African violet)

Warm. A charming small plant with pleasant fleshy green leaves and violet-like flowers, mainly pink and purple in color and virtually ever-blooming.

Saintpaulia ionantha is a major parent of the many hybrids that need a winter temperature of 55°F (13°C). The atmosphere should be humid. Always keep the soil moist, without wetting the plant's leaves. Feed fortnightly with liquid manure during the summer.

Propagate from leaf cuttings during the summer. Place in a propagator at 64–70°F (18–21°C). It may also be grown from seed, germinated at the same temperature, but this is mainly for hybridizing.

Sansevieria trifasciata 'Laurentii' (snake plant, mother-in-law's tongue)

Warm or tropical. *Sansevieria trifasciata* is essentially a foliage plant, with narrow, fleshy, pointed and slightly twisted leaves edged with yellow and banded with green.

Below: Saintpaulia is among the most spectacular of plants that can be grown in a greenhouse.

Sansevieria trifasciata 'Laurentii' is nicknamed mother-in-law's tongue.

Minimum winter temperature should be 50°F (10°C). Allow the plant to dry out in the summer between waterings. Feed monthly from May to September.

Propagate from suckers potted up in growing compost.

Senecio (syn. Cineraria) cruenta

Cool. There are numerous varieties which form compact masses of daisy-like flowers from December to May, according to when they were sown, in colors which include white, lavender, blue, mauve, red, pink and various bicolors.

Plant the seedlings in a rich potting soil or soilless growing compost, and keep them at a temperature of 46°F (8°C) from October onwards, during which period the plants should be fed every two weeks with liquid manure and watered – but not over-watered – regularly.

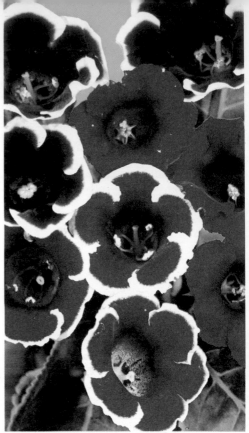

Sinningia speciosa (gloxinia) is essentially a greenhouse plant, with large bell-like flowers.

They can be raised from seed between April and August at a temperature of 55°F (13°C). Grow the seedlings on through the summer in 3 in (7·5 cm) pots in an open frame, shading with muslin during hot spells; bring them into the greenhouse in September.

Sinningia speciosa (gloxinia)

Cool or warm. Gloxinias have large bell-like white, pink, blue and red flowers during summer and autumn.

Provide the plants with a humid atmosphere, keep them moist and feed with liquid manure weekly from the formation of buds until the last flower falls. As the leaves turn yellow, cease watering, gradually remove the dead flowers and leaves, remove the

There are few more colorful or easier to grow pot plants for greenhouses than *Senecio cruenta*.

corms from the pot and store them in a dry place at 50°F (10°C). Re-start growth in early spring by plunging the plants into growing compost and placing in a propagator.

Gloxinias are either propagated from seed at a temperature of 60°F (15°C), or else they can be propagated from leaf cuttings.

Stephanotis floribunda (Madagascar jasmine)

Warm or tropical. This evergreen, twining shrub has dark green leaves and heavily perfumed, white, waxy flowers from May to October.

It can be grown in large pots or in the greenhouse border, from either of which it is trained up wires or a cane framework. The best winter temperature is 55°F (13°C), but from April until late October it should not fall below 64°F (18°C) for long

Right: Strelitzia is grown for its large, dramatic flowers. *Below.* Stephanotis floribunda is an exquisite, sweetly scented climbing plant for greenhouses.

(a higher temperature does not matter). Keep the plant just moist in winter. While it is growing give ample water and maintain a humid atmosphere. Provide a little shade during the summer, otherwise let it have full light. Feed fortnightly with liquid manure from May to September.

Propagate from cuttings of lateral non-flowering shoots in a propagator at 64–70°F (18–21°C).

Strelitzia (bird of paradise flower)

Warm or tropical. *Strelitzia reginae* is an evergreen perennial that yields the most intriguing bird's-head-shaped flowers of green, purple, orange and blue in April and May.

In winter it needs a temperature of 50°F (10°C) and to be kept nearly dry. Water freely during spring and summer. Prevent scorching of the leaves by shading, and ventilate when necessary to lower the summer temperature to 64–70°F (18–21°C). Pot on or re-pot every second year in March. Liquid-feed the plant every two weeks while it is growing.

Propagate by detaching single-rooted shoots after flowering and potting them up in growing compost. Strelitzia is also raised from seed which should be germinated at 64–70°F (18–21°C).

Streptocarpus
(cape primrose)

Cool or warm. These are showy hybrids with large, corrugated leaves and flowers of red, purple and white between May and October.

During winter streptocarpus requires a

Below: Tradescantia fluminensis 'Variegata' are some of the most easily grown of greenhouse trailing plants.

Above: Streptocarpus hybrids are very popular greenhouse plants.

temperature of 50°F (10°C), and then 55°F (13°C). Water freely during the growing period and sparingly in winter. Shade the glass, and ventilate when necessary during the summer. Feed with weak liquid manure fortnightly from May to September. Propagate streptocarpus by division or leaf cuttings, or sow seeds.

The handsome, large, white flowers of *Zantedeschia aethiopica* are very useful for flower arranging.

Tradescantia fluminensis

Cool or warm. This species has leaves that turn pale purple underneath in bright light. 'Quicksilver' is a silver variegated variety. Tradescantia needs a winter temperature not lower than 45–50°F (7–10°C). The plant should be kept just moist. Water freely during the growing season. Position in good light, out of direct sunlight. Re-pot annually in April. Feed with weak liquid manure fortnightly from May to September.

This plant is easily propagated from tip cuttings at 61°F (16°C).

Zantedeschia aethiopica (Arum lily)

Cool or warm. The arum lily has beautiful large white flowers with a conspicuous yellow spadix and large, green, slightly glossy arrow-shaped leaves. It flowers from March to June, according to the temperature in which it is kept.

Arum lilies are propagated from offsets, which may be taken at the time of re-potting the plant.

11 Frames and other plant protectors

Like greenhouses, garden frames and other kinds of protection, such as Hotkaps, give another dimension to gardening. Although the principle embodied is quite an old one, it remains very popular and is still being developed as a current technique. All have common functions, but there are marked differences in the manner in which they are used. They afford protection to plants against adverse weather conditions and can extend their growing season.

Garden frames

A garden frame is very complementary to a greenhouse. There are, for example, many greenhouse subjects that can spend much of their time under a frame, and thus release space in the greenhouse. In fact, younger plants often flourish better in its cooler environment. Also, after flowering, plants can be transferred to a frame from the greenhouse to dry off and rest. A frame is essential for hardening off bedding plants, and for raising and propagating many types of plant. When no greenhouse is available, a garden frame can be heated by means of warming cables, or by the traditional method, animal manure.

Garden frame structure Basically, frames have base walls made of tongued and grooved lumber, metal, cement blocks, or plastic, on the top of which is fixed a sash, which is a wooden or metal frame glazed with glass or plastic.

Choosing garden frames The frame's purpose will dictate what type should be bought or constructed. For raising seedlings, rooting cuttings and growing vegetables such as lettuce or early carrots, the frame need not be very high. The more usual lean-to type, with a height of 18 in (45 cm) at the back and 12 in (30 cm) at the

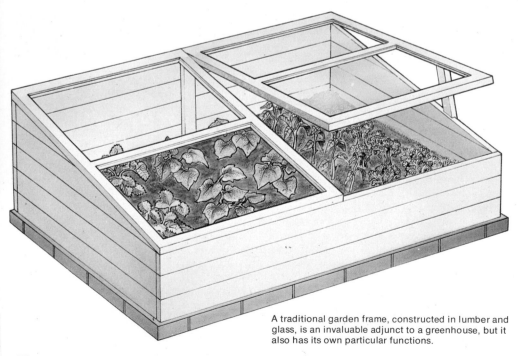

A traditional garden frame, constructed in lumber and glass, is an invaluable adjunct to a greenhouse, but it also has its own particular functions.

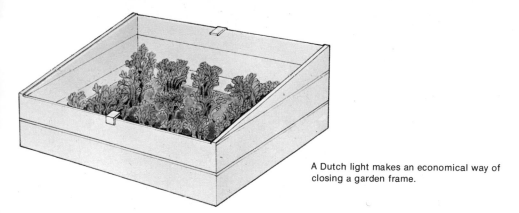

A Dutch light makes an economical way of closing a garden frame.

front, will therefore serve. This type is usually fitted at the top with a 6 ft x 4 ft (2 x 1·25 m) or 14 x 4 ft (1·25 x 1·25 m) sash that slides up and down on runners.

For higher-growing plants, such as pot plants, snap beans and cauliflowers, more depth is needed and a span-roof frame should be chosen. This is like a mini-greenhouse, with sash that can be opened, sloping from the side walls to a central ridge.

Perfectly adequate frames can be improvised by the handy gardener utilizing discarded windows. The dimensions of the frame must be built to fit the window frame. Quite practical but temporary frames can be put together with a couple of layers of polyethylene sheeting stapled to a frame serving as the sash.

Siting garden frames The site should be well-drained, and not too near buildings or trees, which will deprive the frame of light and could be the cause of damage from falling debris. A wooden-base frame should be stood on a course of bricks. Lean-to frames are best placed against a wall facing south or south-west.

Cleanliness and ventilation It is important to keep frames free of rotting debris, and the glass clean. Good ventilation is essential when frames are in use. Both temperature and air ventilation are controlled by opening and closing the sash.

Shading Some form of shading, for example, a thin lime wash on the sash, should be provided during hot weather.

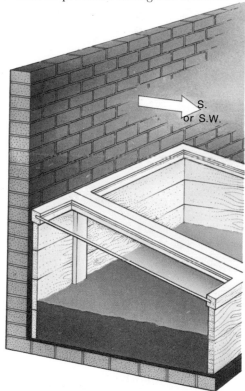

A lean-to frame should be positioned against a south or southwest-facing wall.

57

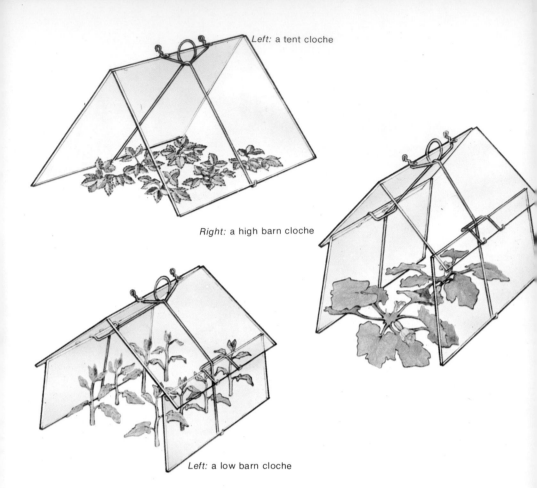

Left: a tent cloche

Right: a high barn cloche

Left: a low barn cloche

Choosing cloche-like protectors

Most American gardeners are familiar with the term 'cloche', used to describe tent-like glass protectors of individual garden plants or even whole rows of plants. The practice is a common one in Europe and the British Isles, especially in those regions where springs are cool and wet, and summers short and equally cool.

About the closest Americans have come to the use of a cloche has been with the Hotkap, a dome-shaped enclosure of waxed paper used as a temporary protector of tomatoes, eggplants, peppers, melons, squash and a few other crops in spring. Hotkaps come in five different sizes, the highest being 12 in (30 cm). Hotkaps, when firmly anchored in the soil, give plants from three to five weeks of protection from frost, wind storms, burning sun, birds and insects. A slit is usually cut in the top for

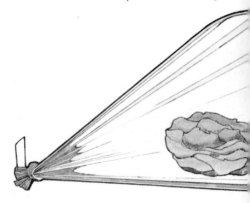

ventilation, either at the time of placement or a week or so later, depending on the crop and the climate.

With the advent of plastic and the low cost of polyethylene sheeting, gardeners are starting to adapt protection techniques more akin to the cloche concepts. The tunnel cloche is one adaptation now available to American gardeners, who can devise their own by bending a series of wires over rows of plants, bush snap beans, for example, and then stretching polyethylene over the wire. Or complete kits can be purchased from mail-order seed and nursery houses under various trade names, such as Spring Jumper, Gard-N-Gro, etc. A tunnel cloche can be used in spring to give quicker growth and the same protection as does a Hotkap, and can also be used in fall as protection from early frosts.

Other variations of the cloche can be devised from such kitchen left-overs as plastic milk and cider bottles. The bottom of the container is simply cut off, the cap removed for ventilation and the container then pressed well into the soil over the plant.

Although protectors of all kinds are mostly used by American gardeners on food crops, they can be useful for ornamental plants, too. Care should be taken to see that the soil beneath the protectors is moist before the protector is placed.

Below: The plastic tunnel, a more recent innovation, protects a row of plants as effectively as the older types of cloche and is more easily stored.

Getting the best from cloches

Whatever type of cloche is used, it is wise to have the rows running away from buildings and trees, so that no shadows are cast.

Advance planning is important, and the site must have been well prepared and previously fertilized. To give the ground time to warm up before planting or sowing it is also necessary to place the protection in position two weeks or so beforehand. Doing this will certainly aid germination and will help any plant to get away to a better start.

Watering isn't the problem it would at first appear, for, if the ground is thoroughly watered first, the water that runs down the sides should be sufficient to keep the ground adequately moist beneath. It helps to make a shallow gulley on each side of the tunnel or cloche which will serve to channel the water.

From time to time it will be necessary to get at the plants of course – for thinning and

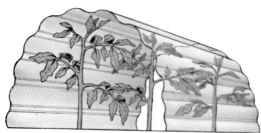

Above: A plastic cloche has the advantage over glass cloches of being unbreakable and less dangerous in gardens where young children play.

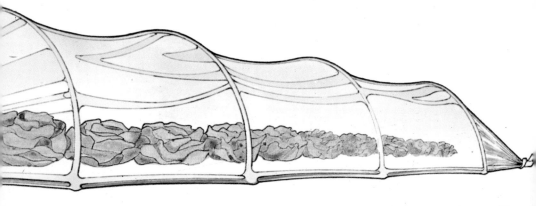

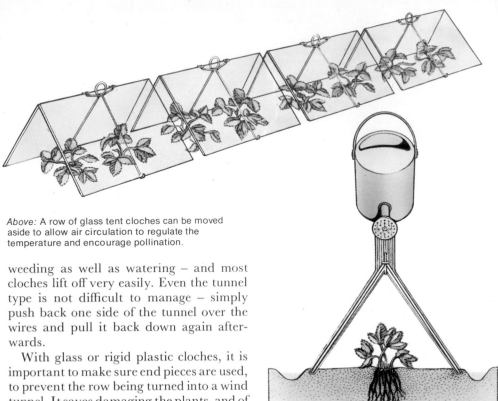

Above: A row of glass tent cloches can be moved aside to allow air circulation to regulate the temperature and encourage pollination.

weeding as well as watering – and most cloches lift off very easily. Even the tunnel type is not difficult to manage – simply push back one side of the tunnel over the wires and pull it back down again afterwards.

With glass or rigid plastic cloches, it is important to make sure end pieces are used, to prevent the row being turned into a wind tunnel. It saves damaging the plants, and of course the end pieces will also keep the warm air in.

While crops are growing many of the rules that apply to greenhouses are equally valid for cloches. Ventilation is important as the days grow warm – and indeed some crops may also require that pollinating insects have unhindered access. And, like greenhouses, the glass (or plastic) should be kept clean if maximum light is to benefit the plants. Equally, plants may need some shade from very hot sunshine, and the shading washes for greenhouses can be used. Normally, however, cloches tend to be used to extend the growing season and shading is not likely to be very necessary early or late in the season.

Cloches and frames do more than provide a snug micro-climate in which plants can flourish, much as they would in a greenhouse. They also offer protection from

Plants under cloches are watered from overhead so that water flows into gullies on either side.

birds, which can be very useful with, say, an early crop of lettuce; by the time they have to be ventilated enough that they might allow birds in, the plants are usually sufficiently established to withstand the onslaught.

Because the plants grown in these mini-greenhouses tend to be lush and tender, it is important that the plants are only very gradually exposed to the full outside air if the cloches are to be moved on to another crop.

Remember, too, that protection in the fall can bring results just as worthwhile as protecting crops in the spring.

12 Common greenhouse pests and diseases

In the tables below are described some of the troubles that affect greenhouse plants.

Pests

Pest		Susceptible plants	Signs	Remedies
Aphids (greenfly)		Most	Stems, leaves and buds are swarmed with green larvae. Young growth disfigured.	Spray with malathion, diazinon or resmethrin.
Caterpillars		All	Eaten or curled leaves.	Spray with diazinon or carbaryl.
Cyclamen mites		Cyclamen, African violets, and others	Deformed, stunted growth. Black buds.	Spray with kelthane.
Leaf hoppers		Many	Coarse mottling on upper sides of leaves.	Regular fumigation. Spray with resmethrin.
Leaf miners		Chrysanthemums, cinerarias and other pot plants	Leaves tunnelled.	Regular fumigation. Spray with malathion.
Mealy bugs		Many	Small tufts or waxy wool appearing on leaves and stems.	Spray with dimethoate or malathion.
Red spider mites		Many	Yellow mottling on upper side of leaves. Yellowing of leaves, then bronzing and ultimately leaf fall.	Regular fumigation. Spray with dimethoate or kelthane.
Scale insects		Many	Leaves and stems become sticky; closer examination shows that stems are covered with brown, yellow or white scales.	Spray with malathion or petroleum emulsion.

Pest		Susceptible plants	Signs	Remedies
Snails and slugs		Many	Chewing damage, especially tender growth. Hide under benches and pots during day.	Special slug bait or deep saucers filled with beer.
Thrips		Various species attack many plants	Distortion occurs.	Spray with malathion.
Weevils		Begonias, cyclamen, vines pelargoniums, primulas, etc.	Plants collapse owing to roots being eaten.	Add diazinon to potting soil, according to package directions.
White flies		Many	Underside of leaves infested with white scales, which are immature white flies.	Regular fumigation, or spray with resmetherin.

Diseases

Disease	Susceptible plants	Signs	Remedies
Blackroot-rot	Many	Rotting of the roots and tissues at the crown. Tissues become black.	Water plants with a solution of captan.
Bud drop	Camellias, stephanotis, etc.	Buds drop off before flowering.	Often caused by dry soil condition at bud formation; sometimes caused by extremes of day and night temperatures.
Carnation stem rot and die-back	Carnations	Stems rotting.	Control by spraying stock plants with captan two weeks before and while taking cuttings.
Damping off	All seedlings and cuttings	Collapsing and dying.	Overcrowding, growing in too wet conditions, in compacted soil or in too high a temperature should be avoided. Check attacks by watering seedboxes with captan.
Foot rot	Calceolaria, geraniums, etc.	Blackening and rotting at the base.	May be caused by contamination of water supply from a tank or barrel. Add small pea-size lump of copper sulphate or crystals of potassium permanganate until water just pink, to purify.

Disease	Susceptible plants	Signs	Remedies
Gray mold (botrytis)	Most greenhouse plants	Grayish, velvety fungus on leaves, etc., with ultimate decay.	Remove and burn infected parts. Give good ventilation. Spray with captan or benomyl.
Gummosis	Cucumbers, melons	Distorted fruits, sunken spots, exuding gummy liquid, which becomes covered with dark green fungus.	Ventilate and heat adequately. Burn all infected fruits. Spray with zineb or captan.
Leafspot	Primulas, anthurium, dracaenas, etc.	Pale brown, irregular spots.	Remove dead leaves. Spray with captan, maneb or zineb.
Mildew, downy	Lettuce and ornamental plants	White tufts or downy patches, usually on underside of leaves.	Spray with thiram.
Mildew, powdery	Carnations, cucumbers, grapes, chrysanthemums, etc.	White powdery coating on stems and leaves.	Spray with benomyl.
Physiological disorders	Many plants	Brown and yellow blotches on leaves, browning of leaf tips, splitting of leaves, dropping of leaves, etc.	Generally improve conditions. Give adequate watering; attend to nutriments, correct temperature, humidity levels, and so on.
Rust	Cineraria, carnations, beans, apricots	Brown or black spots on foliage.	Encouraged by high humidity, which should be controlled by increasing ventilation; destroy leaves and badly infected plants. Spray with thiram and zineb.
Tomato leaf mold	Tomatoes	Yellow blotches on upper sides of leaves; purple-brown mold underneath.	Good cultivation and a maximum temperature of 70°F (21°C) usually prevent trouble. Also spray with zineb, or maneb.
Virus diseases	Tomatoes, strawberries, narcissi, chrysanthemums, cucumbers, carnations, etc.	Wide range of symptoms includes color changes in leaves and stems and flowers, distortion, wilting, stunting of growth, etc.	Destroy any suspect and seedy plants for which there is no obvious explanation for ill-health. Virus disease is spread by common greenhouse pests, so always destroy them.

Index

aechmea, 5
African violet, 50–1
amaryllis, 45
anemone, 60
anthurium, 5, 34, 63
aphelandra, 5, 24, 34
aphids, 61
apples, 30
apricots, 30, 63
arum lily, 55
asparagus, 60
Aspidistra elatior, 34–5
aubergines, 5, 26, 60
avocado pears, 5
azalea, 50

Barberton daisy, 44
beans, dwarf French, 27, 57, 60, 63
begonias, 5, 35
bellflower, 38
Beloperone guttata, 35–6
bird of paradise flower, 53
blackroot-rot, 62
botrytis, 63
bouvardia x domestica, 36
Brompton stocks, 60
Brunfelsia calycina, 36
bud drop, 62
bulbs, 25, 36–7
busy lizzie, 45–6

cabbage, 60
calceolaria, 37–8, 62
calendula, 60
camellias, 24, 38, 62
Campanula isophylla, 38
Cape primrose, 54
capsicum, 60
carnations, 38–9, 62, 63
carnation stem rot and die back, 62
carrots, 60
cast-iron plant, 34–5
caterpillars, 61
cauliflowers, 57
celeriac, 26
celery, 26, 60
Chamaedorea elegans, 46–7
chlorophytum, 25, 39
chrysanthemums, 6, 9, 18, 21, 39–40, 61, 63
cineraria, 52, 61, 63
Clivia miniata, 40–1
cloches, 56, 57–60
codiaeum, 41
Coleus blumei, 41–2
Columnea gloriosa, 42
composts, 22–3
conservatories, 7, 10
cordyline, 42
corms, 25
crocus, 37
croton, 41
cucumbers, 5, 29, 60, 63
currants, 30

Cyclamen persica, 42

daffodils, 37
dahlias, 5, 25
dieffenbachia, 5, 42
dracaenas, 24, 42–3, 63
dumb cane, 42
Dutch iris, 60

endive, 60
Euphorbia pulcherrima, 43

fertilizers, 22
ficus, 24, 43
figs, 5
flamingo plant, 34
foot rot, 62
frames, garden, 56–7
Francisea calycina, 36
French beans, dwarf, 27, 57, 60
fruit, 30–3, 60
fuchsia, 4, 44

geraniums, *see* pelargoniums
gerbera, 44
gladiola, 60
gloxinias, 52
grapes, 32–3, 63
greenfly, 27, 61
greenhouse culture, 22–5
greenhouses,
  choosing, 9
  construction materials, 8
  fitments and equipment, 17–21
  heating, 14–16
  installing, 10–11
  maintenance, 11
  shading, 13
  shapes, 6–7
  types of, 5
  ventilation, 12
Grevillea robusta, 44–5
grey mould, 63
gummosis, 63

hippeastrum, 45
howea, 47
Hoya carnosa, 45
hyacinths, 37

Impatiens sultanii, 45–6
Indian or indoor azalea, 50
India-rubber plant, 43
irises, 25

jasminum, 46

leaf loppers, 61
leaf miners, 61
leafspot, 63
lettuce, 6, 9, 26–7, 60, 63
lily of the valley, 60

Madagascar jasmine, 53
marantas, 25, 46
mealy bugs, 61
melons, 33, 60, 63

mildew, 63
mother-in-law's tongue, 51

narcissi, 37, 63
nectarines, 5

orchids, 5

painter's palette, 5, 34
palms, 34–5, 46–7
peaches, 5, 30–1
pears, 30
peas, 60
pelargoniums, 47–8
peperomia, 5, 48–9
pests, 61–2
pilea, 24, 49
plants, ornamental, 34–55
Plumbago capensis, 49
poinsettia, 43
porcelain flower, 45
primula, 47–8, 63
propagation, 19–21, 23–5

raspberries, 30
red spider mite, 26, 27, 30, 61
Rhododendron indicum, 50
rhubarb, 27–8
rust, 63

saintpaulia, 50–1
Sansevieria trifasciata, 51
scale insects, 61
Senecio (syn. *Cinereria*) *cruenta*, 52, 61, 63
shrimp plant, 35–6
silk bark oak, 44–5
Sinningia speciosa, 52
slipper flower, 37–8
snake plant, 51
snowdrops, 37
spider plant, 39
Stephanotis floribunda, 53, 62
strawberries, 31, 60, 63
strelitzia, 5, 53
streptocarpus, 54
sweetcorn, 60

tarsonemid mites, 62
thrips, 27, 62
tomatoes, 5, 6, 13, 26, 28–9, 60, 63
tomato leaf mould, 63
Tradescantia fluminensis, 54
Transvaal daisy, 44
tulips, 37

vegetables, 26–9, 60
verticillium wilt, 13
violets, 60

watering, 18–9
weevils, 62
white flies, 62

Zantedeschia aethiopica, 55
zebra plant, 5, 34
zinnias, 60